THE KASSEL RAID
27 SEPTEMBER 1944

This book is dedicated to the airmen of the 445th.

THE KASSEL RAID

27 SEPTEMBER 1944

THE LARGEST LOSS BY USAAF GROUP ON ANY MISSION IN WWII

ERIC RATCLIFFE

AIR WORLD

AIR WORLD

THE KASSEL RAID, 27 SEPTEMBER 1944
The Largest Loss by USAAF Group on any Mission in WWII

First published in Great Britain in 2020 by
Air World
An imprint of
Pen & Sword Books Ltd
Yorkshire – Philadelphia

ISBN 978 1 52677 462 0

Typeset by SJmagic DESIGN SERVICES, India.

Printed and bound in UK by TJ Books Limited.

Pen & Sword Books Limited incorporates the imprints of Atlas, Archaeology,
Aviation, Discovery, Family History, Fiction, History, Maritime, Military, Military
Classics, Politics, Select, Transport, True Crime, Air World, Frontline Publishing, Leo
Cooper, Remember When, Seaforth Publishing, The Praetorian Press, Wharncliffe
Local History, Wharncliffe Transport, Wharncliffe True Crime and White Owl.

For a complete list of Pen & Sword titles please contact

PEN & SWORD BOOKS LIMITED
47 Church Street, Barnsley, South Yorkshire, S70 2AS, England
E-mail: enquiries@pen-and-sword.co.uk
Website: www.pen-and-sword.co.uk

Or

PEN AND SWORD BOOKS
1950 Lawrence Rd, Havertown, PA 19083, USA
E-mail: Uspen-and-sword@casematepublishers.com
Website: www.penandswordbooks.com

MIX
Paper from
responsible sources
FSC
www.fsc.org   FSC® C013056

Contents

Preface

Much has been written over the years on the causes and blame for the disastrous Kassel mission. Like most accidents, it was a set of different circumstances and errors coming together to produce the deadly end result: faulty information on wind speeds and direction caused an overshoot of the IP (initial point); a late turn onto the wrong heading, probably caused by misinterpretation of the ground radar image; the decision to 'stick with it' rather than try to correct the course error – all conspired to put the Liberators of 445th at a place in the sky where, for a brief few minutes, the German Luftwaffe ruled. Those factors combined cost the lives of 115 bomber crew and one fighter pilot on the Allied side, and eighteen Germans.

Between 13 December 1943 and 25 April 1945, the 445th flew 280 missions from Tibenham. They lost 108 aircraft in action and, during that period, 554 aircrew lost their lives. The Kassel mission alone cost more than 25 per cent of their total aircraft losses in combat and more than 20 per cent of their total human losses in just one day of bloody battle.

It is testimony to the extreme bravery of these young men that the day after the Kassel debacle more than ninety aircrew climbed into the ten serviceable aircraft left and went back to where their friends and colleagues had died a day earlier.

The group flew another 112 missions before the end of the war.

We owe them a great debt.

Introduction

In the hot summer of 1975, I was invited to have a glider flight at an airfield called Tibenham. At that time I had never thought about flying, had barely heard of gliding, but decided it was an experience I shouldn't pass up. So, after a lot of driving around rural Norfolk (it was in the days before GPS navigation) I found myself being strapped into the front seat of an ASK 13 glider, hooked by tow rope to a little single-engine Condor tow-plane and then, with an instructor in the back giving the signal, we set off down one of the huge runways and into the blue sky. Forty minutes later, back on terra firma, I couldn't wipe the grin from my face. That was it! I was hooked.

Over the next 44 years a lot changed. In 1975 the airfield was owned by a local farmer, having been bought back from the air ministry in 1962, and Norfolk Gliding club rented it for its operations. It was an uneasy relationship as the NGC had little money, and the farmer was busy asset stripping, selling off the hangars, Nissen huts and starting to rip up and crush the concrete to be sold for aggregate. But in 1975 the airfield itself was still more or less complete, with the runways, perimeter tracks, hard-standings and control tower all there to be explored. During this period I became interested in the history of the place and spent the hours when not flying exploring the various areas and amassing a collection of bits of aircraft and artefacts left behind by the Americans thirty years earlier.

As the years went by, I met lots of American veterans returning either as groups for their UK reunions (including the famous Jimmy Stewart, several times) or individually, usually showing families their old base and local haunts. At one of these reunions I was tasked to look after a group of veterans at a local hotel and sat at dinner one evening next to a tall, greying gentleman who introduced himself as Reg – Reg Miner, a former 445th pilot and survivor who was shot down on the Kassel raid. I listened intently as Reg and a couple of others from his crew recounted their tales and I was amazed – almost spellbound – and from there the seeds of this book were sown.

INTRODUCTION

I started to collect documents and accounts from the veterans as I met them and bought all Aaron Elson's audio CDs – and that was the final motivating factor. Listening for hours to the guys I had met over the years made me open the laptop and start to type.

Tibenham itself survived the onslaught of the concrete crushers and although in that period we lost most of the buildings, including the control tower, nearly all of the hard-stands, the peri-track and the end of one runway, in 1987 the gliding club managed to buy enough of the runways to operate from. Three years later, with help from some Americans, club members and some grant aid, the club managed to acquire the remainder, thus protecting it from being ripped up like so many former airfields in East Anglia.

Our greatest assets are the three large runways – but this brings with it a cost. The asphalt is mainly more than 75 years old and it's starting to show its age, weeds abound on the areas that are little used and potholes appear regularly. So, for every copy of this book sold, a donation will go towards runway maintenance as a living memorial to those 554 airmen who took off from them more than 75 years ago – but never landed on them again.

Eric Ratcliffe, Tibenham Airfield, Norfolk, UK, 2019

Foreword by Linda Dewey

I was 6 years old when I first heard about the Kassel Mission. At that time, ten years after the mission, I only learned my dad's story. I would hear many more equally dramatic stories decades later, long after I grew up.

Dad had been a B-24 pilot in the war. He often told my sister and I bedtime stories before we said our prayers each night. On this particular night, the nightstand lamp between our twin beds was turned off. Ambient light from the hallway showed his silhouette as his hands simulated airplanes flying in formation, thumbs and pinkies spread out for the wings as he spoke.

He told us about a terrible air battle when he had nine crewmen aboard and they suddenly had five enemy fighters on their tail. They were hit over and over, and some of his men were wounded before friendly fighters blessedly appeared, scaring off the enemy. The battle left his plane in tatters, and he had to drop out of what was left of the formation.

This next part is where the prayers came in. In America, his mother woke up, turned on the light and said, 'Something's the matter with Billy.' She began to pray.

Deep in enemy territory, Dad, too, prayed and prayed. Suddenly – he told us that night as we lay in our cosy beds – he felt completely calm, almost as if someone else had come in to fly the plane through him.

It took two and a half hours for his plane to limp across enemy territory and over the English Channel. As they dropped below the clouds, 'those beautiful White Cliffs of Dover' came into sight with the long emergency landing strip at Manston. The landing gear did, thankfully, drop down. The tires were fully inflated, he said, and he made his best landing ever.

For my dad, this story had a happy ending. For two-thirds of the 445th Bomb Group's 336 men on that mission, it did not.

Approximately one-third were killed on the Kassel Mission, one-third became PoWs, and the balance eventually made it back to the base. Each had an equally dramatic story. Some of these have been told, some not. You will read many of them here.

The impact

As you will see, the story of the Kassel Mission does not stop with the great air battle. Its impact on its participants afterwards and for those secondary to the battle was immense.

Aside from my grandmother, other women awoke on the other side of the Atlantic the night of the battle. The mother of Kassel Mission air commander Major Don McCoy, who was killed on the mission, woke in the night and couldn't stop screaming. The pregnant wife of pilot Jim Schaen, also killed, felt like her bed was spinning, so bad was her vertigo that night.

Later, in October, families received the first MIA telegrams, followed either by Thanksgiving telegrams saying their son was a PoW, or deadly Christmas visits.

Impact stories coming from that battle are not only from the brave men who fought that day. There were thousands on base. Some of them were alternate crews, but most were ground support – kitchen, operations, command, men who readied and loaded the bombs, mechanics, and ground crews.

At dawn that day, they stood along the runway, counting the planes as they took off, and again lined the runways, sitting on their bikes, to count them back in as they returned. Think of it – when just four of the original thirty-nine B-24s returned. JUST FOUR. They waited for more, but they never showed. Of those four which did make it back safely, only one returned unscathed.

As you will read, the battle nearly wiped out the 445th but, rather than shut the group down, the decision was made to bolster the group. 'Replacements' began arriving that very day, even before the belongings of those who didn't return were removed from their huts. The stories these new men tell of entering the ghostly huts are haunting. This event impacted the group so deeply that for the rest of their lives anyone referring to his time with the 445th would qualify it as 'before' or 'after' the Kassel Mission.

Although the Kassel Mission was only his eighth mission, Dad was soon promoted to captain and became a lead pilot, mainly, as he would tell it in his humble, self-deprecating way, because there were so few pilots left on the base with any experience. After his tour was over, he would become one of two briefing officers – the guys who pulled the sheet off the map showing the target for the day and told them where they were headed. They had also organized the mission overnight.

The Kassel Mission impacted the English who hosted these men at the town of Tibenham – whether they took in laundry, delivered chickens and eggs, tended bar for them at the Greyhound Pub, or worshipped with them at the little church. All were affected deeply when two-thirds of the fliers did not return that day.

The people of central Germany also felt the impact of the battle. As the men and planes fell out of the skies over their homes, they rounded up those airmen lucky enough to wear parachutes – black for Germans, white for Americans. Roughly half landed in what would later be East Germany, and half in West Germany. One boy who was 12 at the time would one day become a battle historian, tracing each crash site to its crew, then locating the players, first in Germany, then in the United States. My father would meet him in 1990.

For the new prisoners of war, their stories continue in prison hospitals and stalags, as you will see.

Many who returned to the base to serve after the battle did not survive the war. Dad promoted his co-pilot because of his excellent performance on the Kassel Mission, but later he and the navigator were killed on a mission on 26 November 1944. The Hunter Crew, which crash landed in France on 27 September, transferred subsequently to the 389th Bomb Group, only to die on a later mission.

A second Kassel Mission

In 1988, the editor of the *8th Air Force News* put out a call for stories on the Kassel Mission, which, he said, they knew very little about – strange, for the greatest loss for a single group in a day's battle. In response, accounts flooded in not only from Americans, but also from former German fighter pilots who still remembered that battle clearly.

The editor, Roger Woolnough, would call it the greatest response ever to a 'call for articles'.

Dad sent in his account and, when the articles overflowed into a second issue, he wrote to Woolnough and suggested he compile them into a little booklet.

Woolnough's response was, 'You do it!' and he sent Dad everything anyone had ever sent him about the Kassel Mission.

Those letters and accounts in the *8th AF News* were compiled into *The Kassel Mission Reports*, which is still available at kasselmission.org, the website for the Kassel Mission Historical Society, which Dad and other Kassel Mission veterans formed. The organization's original purpose was to raise money for a memorial, an idea which someone suggested in one of the responses to the call for articles. Another purpose would be to get the word out in books and publications.

My father always wanted to meet the airmen he flew against – something about 'honour among airmen'. He wondered whether there might be an appropriate spot in Germany for a memorial. He also suggested it be dedicated to the men on both sides of the battle. German Walter Hassenpflug, the boy who witnessed the lead B-24 crash, had met the man he captured the day after the battle, navigator Frank Bertram. The two had reunited. Hassenpflug knew just the spot for the memorial – where that lead plane had crashed.

To raise funds, the Americans created a non-profit organization, the Kassel Mission Memorial Association, which later morphed into the current Kassel Mission Historical Society (KMHS). Dad was at the helm from its formation in 1989 to 2004, with a great group of Kassel Mission veterans and families to help, but the biggest help of all was my mother, who served as Secretary and Treasurer. The two worked feverishly over the years, organizing and accounting for trips, selling PX items as fundraisers, putting out quarterly newsletters full of accounts in the tradition of the *8th Air Force News*.

I was fortunate enough to work with them from 2002 to 2007, when Dad died. Then Mom and I ran the organization, with support from the board until 2010, when she stepped down. I have been president on and off for several years thereafter, until I stepped down for good in 2018.

In a huge joint effort between the German government, which appropriated the land, the US Army Corps of Engineers, which cleared the site and created the road through the pines, the residents, who planted heather in the new memorial park, the German fliers and American airmen who paid for the great Norwegian rocks to be brought in and for the three bronze plaques listing all the airmen, along with their stories, the memorial was completed.

It happened at a time when the Berlin Wall was coming down, and, on 1 August 1990, 46 years after the Kassel Mission battle, the new memorial was dedicated, and former enemies became friends. The next day, they toured the crash sites, where American airmen and the Germans who met them in the air and on the ground told their stories at each site. Bells rang at one town they visited in former East Germany. These were the first Americans the town had seen since before the Second World War.

In closing

The story of the Kassel Mission battle is epic. It was probably the most concentrated air battle ever, since it involved so many planes in a very small area, and because it was so fast. Quick and dirty, it sent men and planes down in a whirlwind of debris. It ended up being the greatest action of the war for the people living in that area of Germany and for the 445th Bomb Group as a whole.

The mystery of why it happened in the first place remains unsolved.

Until Roger Woolnough called for those accounts of the Kassel Mission, the battle had only been given passing notice in one book – Roger Freeman's *The Mighty Eighth*. Freeman, also a Brit, wrote one paragraph about it.

Since then, with support from KMHS, the Kassel Mission has received more attention, both in magazine articles and in books. However, only a handful of books have been written solely about that particular mission. One of them, which gathered information crew by crew, is currently out of print and is being revised. A few others are in German. I know of no others in English, except for the Kassel Mission Reports and a few works written by the airmen themselves or by their children, relating their personal experiences on the Kassel Mission.

Thank goodness our English friend, Eric Ratcliffe, is so dedicated to this cause. Because of people like him, these men and what happened to them will not be forgotten. This event did happen.

Linda Alice Dewey, former KMHS President
Glen Arbor, Michigan, USA
31 July 2019

The Morning of the Raid

A COLD, damp Wednesday morning – 27 September 1944. It's double British summertime and at 2.30 am there was a squeal of brakes as a Jeep pulled into site seven on the 445th Heavy Bombardment Group's base close to the village of Tibenham, twelve miles south of the historic Norman city of Norwich.

Moving through the more substantial concrete Quonset Huts known as 'Officer Country', using his Bakelite flashlight, the driver, a QC orderly (in charge of quarters) known as 'the Gremlin', entered the huts, waking crews due to fly that day. In the chilly environment, sleepy men would emerge from under blankets to hear the name of the pilot whose crew was rostered to fly that day. Sometimes one, sometimes both crews from the hut would hear the dreaded words such as 'Lieutenants Miner and Schaen crews due to fly this morning, briefing 03:30 hours.'

Second Lt George Collar heard the squealing brakes, but the 27-year-old from Michigan wasn't scheduled to fly that morning. He had a three-day pass in his pocket and so was surprised when the Gremlin told him to get up as he was flying. Collar was originally bombardier of Reg Miner's crew when they had all arrived in June a week after D-day, but then Reg had been made a lead crew so they had replaced George with two specialist radar crewmen and he had become a spare. He now had twenty-eight missions with several different crews in his logbook so, when 2nd Lt Aarvig, the bombardier on Schaen's crew, failed to return from a three-day pass, it was an unfortunate George who was rostered for his 29th and, as it turned out, final mission,

Officers were usually billeted two crews to a hut; pilot, co-pilot, navigator and bombardier together. Some of the officers had been woken even earlier, the lead crews had already been briefed on the day's mission, and as lead crews they had the responsibility of getting the group on target at the correct time.

At other sites more QC orderlies were going through the same ritual, waking the sergeants and technical sergeants who made up the enlisted men of the crews. They were billeted in their own quarters at sites two and three and the site originally built for the WAAF (Women's Auxiliary Air Force) for the RAF. They were housed in corrugated, curved-roof Nissen huts, which weren't quite as spacious as the rectangular concrete Quonsets, but there were still ten guys to the hut, with just a single small coal-fired pot-bellied stove in the centre for heating. But on site four there were a couple of large Nissen huts, which actually housed thirty-six crewmen in each.

Most guys knew they were down to fly and, in a lot of cases, found it difficult to sleep, waiting for the noise of the Jeep's engine, squealing brake and the footsteps of the Gremlin. Those who knew how much fuel was being loaded would take an educated guess at their destination. They all hoped it wasn't going to be a deep penetration raid to the 'Big B' – Berlin. Some of the guys made a quick call into the base chapel, hoping to shift the odds in their favour, taking communion from the Catholic chaplain Father Joe Quinlan. For the other denominations, Captain Taylor Minga as group chaplain officiated.

In the hut of Pilot 1st Lt Jackson C. Mercer's crew, Lt Leo Pouliot, his co-pilot, heard the door creak, followed by shuffling steps as the Gremlin went round the edge of bomb-aimer George Noorigian's bed to get to the light switch. Covering his head with a blanket, Leo tried to catch a few more moments in the sack, shivering at the thought of getting up in the cold English morning air, while the orderly woke up Jackson Mercer, George, and navigator Milton Fandler before turning his attention to the shivering Leo.

Reluctantly rising, Leo dressed and went to the washroom to splash icy water on his face before they all headed off to the mess hall for breakfast. Guys headed for the latrines to ensure bowels and bladders were empty. Intestinal gas could be extremely uncomfortable in unpressurised aircraft at 23,000ft and the extreme cold meant relieving oneself was a major epic to be avoided if at all possible.

There were several messes at Tibenham – separate ones for groundcrew, aircrew, officers and enlisted men – clustered round the communal sites and near the officers' club in sites one and two. Although the fare was, in theory, the same in each, the quality of the cook and mess sergeants varied considerably.

Both officers and enlisted men would resort to bartering. Game in the form of rabbits and pheasants and even the occasional deer were poached from the local area with the issue 45-calibre pistols or shotguns 'borrowed' from the skeet shoot, or other weaponry which included rifles, machine guns, home-made bows and arrows and a crossbow. The resulting game could be swapped for canned goods, like Spam or peaches, or even cans of steak which could then be cooked on the pot-bellied stove. The downside of this was the coal ration for heating the hut diminished more rapidly. It was always severely rationed anyway, so ways were found to 'liberate' it from the wire-fenced and sometimes-guarded compound, usually by stealing a contractor's ladder and waiting for the dead of night when the guard wouldn't be so keen to do his rounds. Bribery and corruption also existed. One mess officer was court-martialled and sent to prison for his dealings with base supplies on the black market, and a large amount of American rations was found hidden in the barn of a local farm.

Joining the line for breakfast, and seeing it was powdered egg rather than the fresh eggs usually served when there was a mission on, Leo settled for a cup of coffee and a peanut butter sandwich, hurriedly eaten as briefing was looming. Texan 2nd Lt Walter Eugene George (who preferred to use his middle name rather than Walter) was co-pilot in 1st Lt Donald Brent's crew. He usually took the wings off his uniform so he could sneak into the ground officers' mess hall as he thought the food was better there than the stuff usually served up in the aircrew officers' mess. But that morning he didn't like the look of what was on offer and just settled for some canned peaches.

Other crew maybe had stronger stomachs. It was a cool morning; you could tell autumn was approaching as co-pilot 2nd Lt Carroll Snidow and navigator Maynard Jones walked through the early-morning darkness to the mess hall, where they had the powdered egg for breakfast and remarked it was 'very good'. Little did Carroll and 'Jonesy' know it was going to be their last good meal for a long time. For 117 guys queuing for breakfast in the messes that morning it was going to be their last meal ever.

Other crews had better luck at a different site. Lt John French's crew was woken earlier – at 02.15 – by Sgt Kelly shaking bomb-aimer Robert Timms and 'Doc' Cochran with the news it was fresh eggs for breakfast. They had a full bomb-load of 500lb demolition bombs and *Asbestos Alice* had 2,500 gallons of gas on board. Dressing quickly they headed out for what was scheduled to be their 30th and last mission. When they arrived in their mess hall they found many guys already seated and a queue forming, with the smell of hot coffee and fresh eggs permeating the room. Getting in line, Doc exclaimed, 'This is real service, the last mission and fresh eggs for breakfast!' Grabbing their food, they sat down with their buddy 'Mac' MacGregor, who was also on his 34th and penultimate mission, and discussed whether 'Big B' was likely to be the target. The fact that Major McCoy was going to lead the group – on top of the bomb and fuel loads – pointed to a 'deep' mission. Mac, a native of Delhi, New York, had completed nearly two years of his aeronautical degree before the army drafted him as a combat engineer, but after a few months he was transferred to the 8th Air force as a trainee bombardier. He arrived at Tibenham with the Bud Williams crew, who flew their first mission on D-Day, 6 June. Now, nearly four months later and having flown with six different crews as a lead bombardier, he was going to fly with his best friend Carl's crew. As he forked the last of his egg into his mouth he contemplated he should have finished his missions by now, but he had been caught by the increase from 30 to 35 missions before getting shipped home. So he thought: 'Just one more after this 'milk run' and it will all be over for me.' Unfortunately he didn't know German fighter pilots would have a different idea.

Not all the crewmen in the mess hall were scheduled to fly. Lt John Steinbacher, one of the original pilots to land at Tibenham, had done his twenty-five missions and then, waiting while 'strings were pulled' to be transferred to fighters, had volunteered to do another five. He often got up early and went to get fresh eggs for breakfast even if not listed to fly that day and, being an 'old hand', he would pass on tips and tales to the new crews with remarks like: 'When the Flak is black powder puffs, its gone off and isn't going to hurt, but when the bursts have yellow centres they are getting close. But don't worry, because you'll never see the one that gets you!' John was one of the lucky ones to complete his thirty missions and he got his wish to pilot fighters, flying a P51 Mustang. Unfortunately his luck was soon to run out when John met his end doing a 'beat up' at his old bomber base at Tibenham on 9 December 1944. Flying a Mustang and celebrating his first fighter kill, he got into a high-speed stall and crashed just south of the airfield, near Tivetshall Saint Margaret Church.

Some crewmen, in the hut which housed the officers of the Hansen and Pearson crews, didn't make breakfast. Pilot 1st Lt Ralph Pearson had turned over and gone back to sleep. Waking a few minutes before briefing he and several others frantically scrambled to get dressed and arrived just in time to stand at the back as the olive-green panel door was closed behind them and briefing started.

Out on the airfield ground crews were already hard at work, pulling through the propellers to make sure oil hadn't drained down into the bottom cylinder heads while the engine sat idle, which could lock the cylinder and damage the engine. Crews were also bombing and fuelling their aircraft,

445th Crews at a briefing at Tibenham airfield. (Norwich Library archives)

like the well-worn green-painted *Mairzy Doats,* and the newer, unpainted *Patches* and *Patty Girl.* Among them, on stand number 32, the cold, grey bare-aluminum shape of 42-50383 B-24 H-25 *King Kong* was filled with 2,500 gallons of fuel and six 1,000lb general-purpose bombs as it waited for Lt Baynham's crew. On stand 20, No. 331 *Percy* was waiting for 1st Lt Krivik's crew, and over on stand 36 stood the dull-grey aluminium fuselage of the *Sweetest Rose of Texas,* adorned with great artwork, waiting for 1st Lt Paul Swofford and his crew to bring her to life. First Lt Joe Johnson alighted at hard-stand 14 to see the beautiful, brand-new and immaculate *Fridget Bridget* glistening in the early morning dew.

The ground crew worked tirelessly, S/Sgt/Gunner John Robinson recalled: 'If it was not for them we could not have won the war. They worked 20 out of 24 hours a day. Highly-dedicated to the crew they kept flying. Our crew chief babied us and the aircraft like a mother hen.'

Over in the bomb dump on the extreme western side of the airfield, Corporal Joseph A. Gerety Jr, a member of the 1826 ordnance attached to 445th, had been up all night assembling the thirty-seven bomb loads for the aircraft, consisting of six 1,000lb bombs for all the aircraft except the lead

5

Most maintenance was performed on the hard-stands in all weathers. (© Art Shay Archive)

crews – which carried 500-pounders – which meant nearly 250 bombs had to have their fuses screwed in and the safety pins inserted to stop the little propellers from turning (when the bombs were dropped these spun in the airflow and armed the bomb). Then the bombs had to be loaded onto trollies and towed to each of the dispersals for hoisting into the B-24's bomb bay. By the time the aircrews were at briefing, the ordnance guys were heading for a well-earned meal and bed.

Although it was called Tibenham, most of the base buildings and living quarters on Station 124 were actually in the parishes of Aslacton and Great Moulton. Built in 1941/2 by W. and C. French Ltd, the Class A airfield was opened in 1943 with three standard concrete and tarmac runways; the primary of 2,000 yards and two secondary each 1,400 yards long. They were all the standard 50 yards wide. In addition, there were 35 'frying pan' hard-stands and a further 17 'spectacle' hard-stands. Two T2-type hangars were built for indoor maintenance.

Since the construction of the airfield, the base had even changed the demographics of the village, as the access road to the base and the villages to the east had been asphalted. This meant the original route from Tibenham village to the railway station at Tivetshall, passing both the church and the pub, was just a muddy track and now cut off by the airfield runways anyway, so it had fallen into disuse, and both the pub and the church entrances now faced the wrong way from the new highway.

In the USA a new bomber group was being formed; the general order to bring the 445th Heavy Bombardment Group to life was issued.

> Our Bombardment Group had the usual, unexciting beginning which was typical of all military units—it was born on paper. The only labor pains were probably suffered by the clerk who typed the General Orders, perhaps at the end of the day's work when in a hurry to go on pass.

GENERAL ORDERS)   HEADQUARTERS SECOND AIR FORCE
:   Fort George Wright, Washington
NO ....46)   April 1, 1943

SECTION VI

1. Pursuant to instructions contained in immediate action War Department letter AG 320.2 (3-19-43) OB-I-AFDPU-M, March 20, 1943, subject: "Constitution and Activation of Certain Army Air Forces Units", the following units having been constituted and assigned to Second Air Force are activated as indicated, effective April 1, 1943:

Unit	Station of Activation	Table of Organization	Source & Size of Cadre
Hq. 445th Bombardment GP (Hv)	AAB, Gowen Fld, Boise, Idaho	1-112 (7/1/42)	to be
700th Bombardment Sq (Hv)		1-117 "	announced
701st Bombardment Sq (Hv)		1-117 "	in
702nd Bombardment Sq (Hv)		1-117 "	separate
703rd Bombardment Sq (Hv)		1-117 "	communication

* * * * * * * *

2. The tables of organization listed above will be used as guides in the organization of these units; specific authorization of enlisted grades will be published in a separate communication.

* * * * * * * *

8. Army Air Forces Regulations 15-107, Dec. 12, 15-108, Dec. 15, 1942, and Technical Order 00-25-3 will be complied with immediately by station commanders at stations of activation.

By command of Major General Johnson:

NATHAN B. FORREST,
Brigadier General, G.S.C.
Chief of Staff

THE KASSEL RAID, 27 SEPTEMBER 1944

Station Adjutant Rudolf Birsic tells the story of the group's inception:-

A few weeks passed after activation before personnel in any appreciable numbers were finally transferred to the Group, and these were largely cadre men to form the nucleus of the five units making up the Group.

Lt Col Robert H. Terrill was named commander of the Group. A West Point graduate with many years experience in the Army, he soon proved himself to be a thoroughly sincere, efficient, hardworking, and natural leader.

The Deputy Commander was Major David V. Andersen, and the four Squadron Commanders were Captain Irving H. Ward, 700th ; 1st Lt Howard E. Kreidler, 70lst; 1st Lt James C. Evans, 702nd; and Lt Willis B. Sawyer, 703rd. The Group Operations Officer was Captain William W. Jones.

The key Group Headquarters and Squadron personnel, both officer and enlisted, were soon selected, and the operation of the administration of the Group was well under way by the end of April. A few B-24s were assigned, and the 445th Bomb Group began to prepare for war.

At the end of April 1943, a portion of the Group was sent to the Army Air Forces School of Applied Tactics at Orlando, Florida, for combat training. The instructors at this school were supposed to pass on to these selected Group and Squadron men the latest information on aerial warfare. The course consisted of two weeks of classroom instruction and two weeks of living at satellite fields under battle conditions.

These satellite fields were located within a few miles radius of Orlando.

In all, 49 officers and 81 enlisted men of the Group were sent to AAFSAT, as it was known. It wasn't long before its other name came into more popular use – *Snafu*.

These 130 men consisted of both Group and Squadron Commanders; Group Adjutant; Group and Squadron Operations, Intelligence, Engineering, Armament, Ordnance, Communications, and Medical Officers, and Bombardiers and Navigators; Intelligence and Operations Non-commissioned officers; airplane maintenance personnel and combat crew enlisted personnel.

While this portion of the Group was undergoing training in Florida, the remainder at Boise, Idaho, was acquiring further personnel and gaining administrative experience under the Group and Squadron Executive Officers, the Group Sergeant Major, and the Squadron First Sergeants. By the end of May, 1943, the Group strength at Boise alone was over 225 men, representing over 12 per cent of the Group's authorized personnel.

The Bomb Group at that time had an authorized strength of 293 officers and 1507 enlisted men, including personnel for 48 combat crews.

During the first few days of June, all Group personnel from Orlando and Boise proceeded to Wendover, Utah. Here the Group took up training in earnest. At first, the Group and Squadron Headquarters consisted of a few tents along the concrete parking area on which the aircraft were parked, where every time the engines of the B-24s were started up, the papers in the tents were scattered in every direction by the tremendous blasts of air stirred up behind the propellers. Everyone concerned was glad when another Bomb Group moved out of Wendover and our Group was able to take over its offices.

Life at Wendover could hardly be called exciting. The field was just a collection of flimsy huts and some concrete runways located in the salt flats of western Utah on the Nevada border. Civilization was far removed from this forsaken spot. A hotel or two, a sprinkling of homes, a few trees, and seven (!) gambling casinos and cafes, made up the tiny settlement outside the airfield. From a military point of view, the isolation was an incentive to put in more working hours, since there was little to do with a great deal of leisure. Each morning found both officers and enlisted men drilling down on the line. In the late afternoon, everyone went out to the athletic field where an hour's exercise, or more, daily helped to condition the men. Someone had gone out of his way to make certain everything was provided for us – there was even an obstacle course. Each Saturday morning there was a Group parade.

On June 25 we officially began Operational Training. Two days later we learned that the Group was being moved to Sioux City, Iowa, for further training. This was good news to everyone, as it brought to an end our desert exile. On July 5 we were on our way to Iowa. A limited number of officers and men flew there in what planes we had, and the rest proceeded by troop train.

On the evening of July 7 the troop trains arrived at Sioux City, and in short order the Group was functioning smoothly in spite of the Iowa heat. We were fortunate in being able to take over the former Wing Headquarters, since that Headquarters had moved to Gowen Field.

The big war news those days was the invasion of Sicily. The same day we learned this – July 10, 1943 – we were visited by General Arnold, Commanding General of the Army Air Forces. On July 19, we learned Rome had been bombed for the first time.

We gained many new combat crews as well as various types of ground personnel, so that rapidly we were approaching our authorized strength. We still did not have a great many planes, but those we did have were getting lots of flying time and giving our maintenance men plenty of experience. We did not drill as often as at Wendover, and the parades and reviews stopped completely once intensive training had begun. There were still calisthenics and athletics for conditioning, plus other necessary warfare training ranging from the smells of chemical warfare to the stings of the Medical Department's shots. A great deal of work had to be done on personnel records, not the least of which was reclassification, which involved a great deal of red tape. It was no small task to put the right man in each spot; personnel changes and shifts were being made continually, although training could never be slighted and never was. Colonel Terrill personally checked the status of training, personnel, and equipment, and he was completely in touch with the progress and any deficiencies of the Group.

The Sioux City heat at this time was terrific. The only redeeming feature of all the sunshine was the very healthful tans everywhere in evidence on the majority of the Group men. Colonel Rush, the Wing Commander, visited us on July 30, and such a visit was always good for some juicy rumors. Probably our most publicized personnel addition, which occurred in the early days of August, was the assignment of Captain

Jimmie Stewart as 703rd Bomb Squadron Operations Officer. The novelty of having this movie star in our midst soon wore off, especially since he proved himself to be a hard-working, sincere, 'regular' fellow.

Leaves and furloughs were uppermost in everyone's mind, for our time in the States was growing shorter every day. The announcement on August 6 that ten-day leaves were authorized caused no little excitement, but it was short-lived. In fairness to those who had already had only seven days' leave and because there was not much time left in which to cram so much training, Colonel Terrill ruled that seven days' leave would be the Group policy.

Overseas physical exams were being given about this time, but they were hardly an accurate forecast of the date of our departure for overseas service. On August 13 we received by teletype authorization to increase our combat crew strength to 70 crews. This meant an increase in personnel of 88 officers and 132 enlisted men. Two major personnel changes about this time were the assignment of Major Paul Schwartz as Deputy Group Commander and Captain James Stewart as Commander of the 703rd Bombardment Squadron.

August 26, 1943, ushered in a period of disaster for the Group. It was a grim foretaste of things to come. One of our ships on a night training flight crashed, and the nine men aboard were killed. On Thursday, September 2, a few minutes before midnight, another ship went down in flames, killing all ten crew members. The plane crashed just a short distance from the Base, and many persons saw it go down in flames. We had hardly recovered from the shock of this tragedy when about noon on Saturday, September 4, we received news of a third crash, which claimed eight victims. It was no wonder that we were beginning to feel jinxed, and a bit jumpy.

Fortunately, this proved to be the last accident of our Operational Training days in the States. Early September saw the arrival of our first final type of B-24 Hs. These were the planes which the Group would take overseas for combat use. With the news of Italy's surrender on September 8, there were many persons with visions of the end of the war in Europe.

The end of our training in the States was rapidly approaching, but not before further drastic changes were made. Three of the Squadrons were moved to satellite bases. The 700th Squadron was stationed at Mitchell, South Dakota. The 701st Squadron was delighted to find its new home was Scribner, Nebraska, which was a unique field in at least one respect and that was in its expert camouflage work – it was quite difficult to detect the Base from the air. Watertown, South Dakota, was the new Base for the 702nd Squadron. Group Headquarters and the 703rd Squadron remained at the Sioux City Air Base.

Still other major personnel changes followed. The new Group Intelligence Officer was Captain Donald S. Klopfer, of the New York Publishing Firm Random House, and partner of Bennett Cerf. Major Carl Fleming replaced Captain O'Brien as 700th Squadron Commander. Switches were made in various Squadron Intelligence Officer positions, as well as Squadron Administrative Officers and First Sergeants. Captain Taylor Minga became the new Group Chaplain and Lt Leland Simpson the new Group Bombardier.

On the night of October 3, 1943, a notice appeared on Group Bulletin Boards to the effect that we were restricted to the base after 0001 hours on October 7. The notice gave explicit instructions on how to send home our baggage.

At a Staff Meeting the following morning our date of departure was announced. For the next 48 hours everyone was busy stenciling his equipment, baggage, and clothing with his organization shipment number, as well as his name, rank, and serial number. Once the movement began, Group Headquarters and the Squadrons would be designated by only a code number for security reasons. Each organization had its own code number. The big news of October 9 was the fact that new orders had been received; our plans had been changed. Colonel Terrill announced the next day at another Staff Meeting that our training had been extended ten days. We had to make up certain training deficiencies in that time.

On October 11 Colonel Terrill learned that he had been promoted to full Colonel, with date of rank as of July 30.

It was a fitting honor that he be allowed to start overseas bearing his full authorized rank. He had worked hard and loyally, and we were all proud of him.

The last overseas shots were administered to Group Personnel on October 18; our Headquarters were overrun with all types of inspectors for the next day and a half; and on October 20 at 6:30 P.M. one troop train left Sioux City, as three others from the Satellite Bases departed almost simultaneously, all bound for Camp Shanks, New York. Sixty-two combat crews and 248 other ground and flying personnel who made up the Air Echelon were left behind to proceed by air, going by way of Florida, Puerto Rico, Brazil, West Africa, and thence to England. Eight combat crews for whom there were no planes traveled with the ground troops. An advance party of four officers had left several days previous (*sic*) by air to proceed directly to our overseas base. They were Lt Col Malcolm Seashore, Group Executive Officer; Major William W. Jones, Group Operations Officer; Captain Donald S. Klopfer, Group Intelligence Officer; and Captain Howard L. Davis, Group Communications Officer.

After spending a day keeping out of sight, the ground echelon finally sailed about 5:30 P.M. on Wednesday, October 27, on board the QUEEN MARY out of New York. We were fortunate in escaping any exceptionally rough seas, and thus there were not too many incidents of seasickness. We dropped anchor in Firth of Clyde off Gourock, Scotland, about 9:30 A.M. on November 2, 1943, after an unescorted and uneventful voyage. We had to spend another day on the QUEEN MARY, but the next morning at 10 A.M. we began to debark onto a lighter which took us to Gourock. Here we boarded a train, which proceeded through Glasgow, Edinburgh, and down the East coast of England, finally arriving at what we learned was Tivetshall Junction in the early morning of November 4. In the pitch dark of the blackout it was impossible to see what our new home was like.

Birsic, Rudolph J., *The history of the 445th Bombardment Group (H) (unofficial)* (1947)

The ground crews had been shipped over to Britain on Cunard's transatlantic liner *Queen Mary*, which had been converted to a troopship. The *Queen Mary* and her sister ship *Queen Elizabeth* ran throughout the war, transporting up to 18,000 troops at a time.

The liner arrived in Gourock on 2 November and in the early hours of 4 November the men arrived at Tivetshall railway station for the short march down Station Road to the unfinished muddy site in the deepest Norfolk countryside. The plan was to send the air echelons a couple of weeks later via the northern route but, due to heavy losses and bad weather, they were ordered to use the southern route down the east coast of the USA, so they travelled across the Caribbean, South America and to North Africa, and started to arrive in Norfolk from 18 November 1943. There was tragedy before they arrived when *Sunflower Sue*, the aircraft of Lt Poor, with his crew and four passengers, was lost somewhere en route over the Caribbean and never heard of again.

All over the different squadron areas, ground crews had constructed huts out of salvaged lumber. The plywood boxes, which contained spare engines, were especially prized to create the shacks which were the only shelters out on the windswept airfield. In England the bike constituted the main form of transport on all bases. Indeed it was routine to see officers, regardless of rank, pedalling around the countryside and cities rather than driving the Willy jeeps all bases used as base transport. The disbursement of the planes

RMS *Queen Mary*, nicknamed 'The Grey Ghost'. (Norfolk Gliding Club archive)

It wasn't until 4 January 1944 that the 445th BG officially took possession of the RAF base at Tibenham in England, with an official handover ceremony. (NARA)

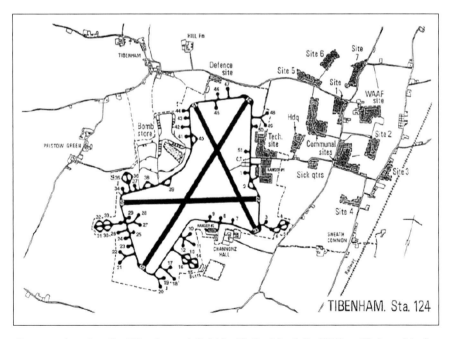

Construction plan for Tibenham airfield in 1943. (Norfolk Gliding Club archive)

Bikes were the essential mode of transport with 89 stolen in April alone – 83 were subsequently recovered. 1826 Ordnance Company Sgts Delancy and Danno. (Courtesy Gerety family)

over a wide area of the base made bicycles a necessity rather than a luxury. Some of the hard-stands were more than a mile from the living quarters and mess halls, so a bike was essential to get around the airfield efficiently. On arrival, many men had been directed into Norwich to buy them from Fred Dodger's shop in Chapel Street. They were amazed at the prices they were charged by the enterprising Fred, who cashed in on a seller's market to the 'overpaid Yanks'. The bikes became prized possessions and could easily disappear if left unattended. When a crew failed to return from a mission, the bikes would quickly be recycled, often auctioned off with the proceeds sent to next of kin.

Maintenance personnel of the 445th BG work on a Consolidated B24 engine at Tibenham. (NARA)

Back in the briefing room, the atmosphere was tense and hushed, the big map with its route to the target hidden behind a curtain. Crews, who by now knew the fuel load, knew it was going to be a deep penetration mission rather than the short 'No Ball' missions they had been doing recently to the V1 'doodlebug' sites on the coast of France. These allowed some crews to get in lots of missions towards their thirty and, together with the fact that these missions were usually well-escorted by the fighter squadrons, made them 'milk runs'. But today they knew it wasn't going to be one of them. Stubbing out their cigarettes, as it was a no-smoking area, the final crews filed in to take their seats, awaiting the 'brass' to arrive. Just before 3.30 am, they all stood as Group C/O William Jones, along with briefing officer Lt Clifford Ackman and the other officers filed in to brief on the weather, intelligence and a host of other details. Then the assembly sat down, the doors were closed and briefing began.

Pulling back the curtain to reveal the large wall map with the route marked, the crews could see the red yarn stretched across the North Sea, over Holland and deep into Germany. Intelligence officer Captain Pallouras (S4) announced the target as the Henschel engine and Tiger tank manufacturing plant at Kassel, Germany. Most of the crews felt a small amount of relief that is wasn't the 'Big B' and, while it was a fairly deep penetration into

17

Germany, with the P51 Mustangs now able to give fighter protection all the way to and from the target, German fighters shouldn't be much of a problem.

Briefing continued with Major Durbon, group Navigation officer, naming Major McCoy and the 700 squadron as the lead crew in the lead squadron, and code words like 'Hambone' for the initial point, 'Lazy Bones' for chaff and others. He told crews the route would avoid flak at Münster and Hamm. Then the Met officer, nicknamed 'Metro Moe' by the crews, moved on to the expected weather of 8 to 10 tenths cloud cover, tops 11,000ft, bombing altitude 23,000ft. Other officers continued the briefing giving out such information as runway in use 21, start-up, taxi instructions and take-off times. Assembly instructions using Buncher 6 and Splasher 5 beacons, radio channels and a host of other information, including that Brussels had just been liberated and the airfield there was available in an emergency. Briefing finished with the synchronization of watches using the 'hack' method, for example: '3:51 coming up in 10 seconds – 5,4,3,2,1, hack.'

With briefing over and dawn fast approaching, some of the crews filed out into the lightening sky and past medical officer Doc Brewer and Chaplin Minga standing by the exit and wishing them a safe trip. A sergeant was handing out phials of morphine, which fitted on the sleeve of a flying jacket. Three small tubes of morphine, with needles attached, were issued and put in the heavy flight-suit jacket, left sleeve pouch, to be used with the following instructions: If wounded – one tube to relieve pain; two tubes to make you sleep; or three to kill yourself. The decision would be yours!

Pilots and co-pilots remained behind for their own briefing, sorting out their headings and timings and checking their weight and balance calculations and a host of other pre-take-off details, while the navigators, bomb-aimers and the radiomen all split off to attend their own briefings in separate rooms.

Recently, most of the ball turrets on Liberators had been removed to save weight and enable increased bomb loads, as the arrival in greater numbers of the long-range P51 Mustang escort fighters had reduced operational losses. This meant the standard crew had dropped from ten to nine, but lead crews also carried specialist radar navigators, and some planes still had a ball turret, which meant Lt Miner's crew, for example, was up to twelve and Captain Chilton's lead aircraft – carrying mission commander Major Don McCoy – was a very unlucky 13. The number of missions had also risen from 25 to 30.

Art Shay, navigator on pilot Cecil Isom's B-24 *Patty Girl*, caught up with the rest of his crew in the locker room. They were already donning the new blue 'Bunny' electrically-heated suits over their thermal underwear and under their heavy, fleece-lined trousers, thick wool socks and felt boot inners,

Navigators plan their courses before a mission. (© Art Shay Archive)

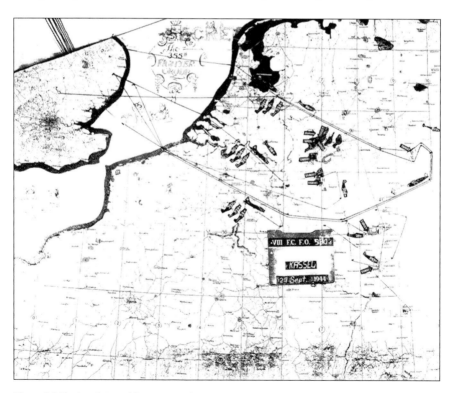

Kassel Mission Map. (Courtesy of KMHS)

before they put on the fleece-lined A6 boots and heavy sheepskin B3 flight jackets. Some men followed instructions and tied their shoes to their harnesses, others didn't bother – a mistake some of them would regret later in the day. Next came a Mae West, a parachute harness and a flying helmet plus oxygen mask – and some guys elected to strap on the optional Colt 45 pistol and harness. A steel helmet and a canteen completed the ensemble.

Aircrew were forbidden from taking any form of ID – apart from their 'dog tags' – and were supposed to make sure they hadn't got cinema or bus tickets on them. Some airmen of the Jewish faith also left behind their 'dog tags', knowing the 'H' for Hebrew was not going to do them any favours if they were shot down in Germany. So, apart from their dog tags, their escape kit consisted of a silk map, foreign currency and a small compass.

It also included photos taken of them wearing civilian clothing. This was to facilitate the making of fake IDs to help with their evasion from occupied territory should they end up in the hands of the resistance. In fact this actually worked in reverse as the Germans could tell which outfit the captured airmen were from just by seeing the attire in the photos, as each bomb group was using the same clothing for all its pictures!

Many of the crew carried lucky charms. Frank Bertram had his baseball mitt, Ray Lemons carried his babies' shoes, others had a selection of talismans like a lucky dollar, a rabbit's foot, or girlfriend's nylon stocking and, for the more religious, a crucifix or communion rosary.

They collected their parachutes from the store, with some guy cracking the inevitable joke about 'bringing it back if it doesn't work'. Parachutes were a mixture of chest, backpack or seat types, depending on position in the aircraft. Collecting their escape kits and 'K' rations and carrying their flight and parachute bags, they all jumped aboard trucks and Jeeps for a lift to the hard-stands where their aircraft sat, still being fussed over by the ground crews. The time had come to go to war.

The furthest hard-stands, belonging to 703 squadron, were arranged around the perimeter track at the southern end of the main runway, well over a mile from the briefing room on the administration site. There were usually two crews in each truck lugging their flight bags and parachutes – flak vests were usually left in the aircraft. Gunners would have got the ammunition for the 50-calibre machine guns already.

Art Shay threw in his gear and jumped up into the olive-drab General Motors six-wheeled cargo truck – widely used for transporting aircrews from mission briefing to the aircraft – to join the rest of the crew for the trip to hard-stand 18 at the extreme end of runway 21. When the truck braked to a halt, the crew jumped down onto the damp concrete where *Patty Girl* stood in the dull-grey, unpainted aluminium known as natural metal finish, with condensation just visible in the pre-dawn light.

All the Second Combat Wing ships were identified by a white stripe on black-painted rudders. The orientation of the white stripe distinguished the three groups composing the Wing: horizontal for the 445th Bomb Group, vertical for the 389th BG and diagonal for the 453rd BG. This had replaced the earlier designation of a white disc with a black letter 'F' on it, the squadron markings painted on the fuselage. RN, the designation for the 703rd squadron, was followed by the individual identification letter in this case E+ for Lt Isom's *Patty Girl*. All the squadrons had their own identifying letters painted on both sides of the fuselage: IS for the 700th Sqd, MK for the 701st Sqd, WV for the 702nd Sqd. The Circle 'F' in the white disc had moved from the tail fins to the top and bottom of both wings.

The briefed runway that morning was '21' which meant 210 degrees was the runway compass heading. So *Patty* had a long taxi round the perimeter

Art Shay and his crew arrive at their hard-stand. (Photo: © Art Shay Archive)

track to the far end of the runway to make her designated slot of 25th on the take-off list.

The deputy lead, the second Liberator to take off, was going to be Captain Web Uebelhoer, so he only had a very short taxi to runway 21 from hard-stand 48. While this saved gas, it also meant more than an hour's extra flying while the flight got into formation – and that could take up to two hours to achieve.

Normally the aircraft formed up behind the garish orange and black-striped assembly ship, the war-weary *Lucky Gordon*, but on this occasion she was at Mount Farm airfield being repaired after a landing accident, so John Chilton's ship would be first to take off and everybody would formate on him.

The trucks circulated the perimeter track, dropping off crews like Reg Miner's onto hard-standing 22, Paul Swofford at 36, William Dewey at 40 and so on until all thirty-nine crews scheduled to fly that day had been delivered to the fifty-one active hard-stands dotted around the perimeter track.

Having loaded their canvas flight bags, equipment and extra ammunition, done the walk-round inspection and signed the form to accept the aircraft from the ground crew chief, the crews stood around indulging in banter. Some joined into little groups to pray, others grabbed the last chance of having a cigarette or taking the opportunity to empty their bladders by 'watering' the grass. For many flyers, waiting for the order to start up was the tensest time of the whole operation. But at around 5.15 am the guys started to climb aboard and take up their positions, starting up the 'putt-putt' auxiliary power unit, plugging in the intercom and heated 'Bunny' suits, and starting to bring the big birds to life. Second Lt James E. Dowling, bombardier on Lt Joe Johnson's crew, crawled in the small tunnel from the flight deck to the nose compartment of a brand new aircraft named *Fridget Bridget*. She wasn't going to remain immaculate for very long in her short history.

On stand 36, Staff Sergeant Jack Laswell put a flak vest on the floor of the left waist gun position for extra protection. He was flying his 15th mission in the lead ship of the 701st Squadron with pilot 1st Lt Donald W. Smith in 42-51710. The 19-year-old gunner had flown with different crews in every gun position, except the top turret, which was usually the home of the flight engineer.

Over on stand 18 Art Shay threw his navigator's bag into *Patty Girl*, hauled himself up though the hatch and settled down at the navigator's table to get his logs organized. Cecil Isom strapped himself in the left-hand seat and, when

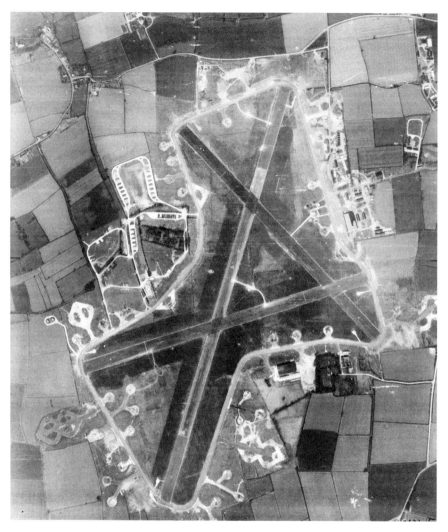

Tibenham Airfield 1946. (Norfolk Gliding Club archive)

Lonnie Justus did the same in the right-hand seat, he started to work his way through the engine start-up checks. Outside, the ground crew removed the tail-support ladder, closed the hatches, and then stood back with fire extinguishers ready. At hard-stand 31A, in the 702-squadron area, the truck dropped off 2nd Lt Howard Jones's crew outside the brand-new aircraft *Rough House Kate*. Unfortunately she wasn't going to stay pristine for much longer.

Sergeant Erickson, radio operator, had been delivered to hard-stand 40 where the aircraft, *Ole Baldy,* a B-24H in olive-drab paint was located.

Patched and battered, she was today the mount of 2nd Lt William F. Golden. Jack Erickson made his way to the flight deck to assume his position, behind the co-pilot seat: 'I pre-flew the radio gear and pre-tuned the transmitter to the assigned frequency. I made sure that a flak suit and a flak helmet had been delivered to my station. I put together the whole outfit. I then tested my oxygen mask and plugged my electrical-heated suit in to make sure it heated properly. Next I checked out my Mae West, to be sure it contained live CO_2 cartridges, and put it on. Next I strapped on my parachute harness and sat down at my radio position all set for another mission.' (kasselmission.org)

At 5.30 am green flares arched through the sky to signal the mission was on and engine start.

Over on hard-stand 7, Lt John French, in the pilot's left-hand seat, started his long list of pre-take-off checks and, with twenty-nine missions already under his belt – just one more to complete – it was almost automatic: undercarriage lever set down; auto pilot and oil dilution off; instruments set; generators off; ignition masters on; mixture set idle cut-off; parking brake, booster pump and main fuel cocks on; throttles set; superchargers off; shutter and gills open. Checks completed, French looked out of the window at the crew chief and held up three fingers to show it was No.3 engine to start. This one was always first because it drove the main hydraulic pump and generators. Getting the thumbs-up from the crew chief that it was clear, John pressed the energize button for twenty seconds while priming and then switched to the mesh setting.

Liberators wait on the perimeter track for start-up signal at Tibenham Airfield. (Norfolk Gliding Club archives)

With that, the 1,200 hp Pratt twin radial belched a big cloud of black smoke and started up.

Running the checks and repeating the procedure until all four engines were running smoothly, the 'putt-putt' could be shut down and, with the hydraulic systems pressurized, the turrets could be rotated to check their movement. Meanwhile the rest of the crew ran through their checks and eyes looked towards the tower for the green flare, and it was time to start the coordinated ballet to get the aircraft to the end of runway 21 in the correct sequence.

Tibenham Control tower 1944.

The Mission

All over the airfield, aircraft started to nod on the front oleos as the brakes were released and then applied, the outer engines powered up to turn the aircraft in the right direction. The first to move was Captain John Chilton from hard-stand 17 in the south-eastern corner of the airfield, now slowly being revealed as the sunrise time of 05:52 was fast approaching. John started the long taxi, anti-clockwise round the western perimeter track to line up first at the threshold of runway 21. Over on the other side of the airfield, Captain Web Uebelhoer, destined to be the deputy lead and the second to take off, started his taxi round the eastern perimeter track clockwise, so the aircraft met and alternated onto the threshold.

With a bomb load of six general-purpose 1,000lb bombs and 2,500 gallons of fuel, the Liberators were close to – and in some cases over – their maximum all-up weight. The procession of aircraft lined up behind each other and, slowly waddling like pregnant ducks, stopping and starting, applying bursts of power then dabs of brakes, all the squadrons lined up. The lead squadron was a mixture of 700 and 703 squadron aircraft, followed by the high high right squadron of 701 Squadron aircraft, followed by 702 in the high right slot, with the rest of 703 squadron in the low left position bringing up the rear.

Missing from the lineup was the first casualty of the day, Lt Rene Schneider. Taxiing from hard-stand 19 he had run off the edge of the ramp, split a tyre and already aborted his trip. The error probably saved the lives of the ten men on board. The 39 scheduled aircraft had now become 38, and more were soon to drop out.

At 05:58 Captain John Chilton had completed his vital-action checks: hydraulic booster pump on; trim set; mixture auto rich; props and superchargers checked; contents, fuel cocks open and booster pumps on; flying controls full and free; flaps set 1/3; autopilot and de-ice off; generators on; gills closed. All the crew checked in to say they were in position and ready to go and the APU had been shut down. Powering up the starboard outer engine and giving a little dab on the left brake brought the aluminium-coloured B-24 J-541H onto the runway. Chilton taxied a few yards to ensure the nose wheel was straight and, at 6 am, he got the green light from the red-and-white checked control cabin, pushed all four throttles forward to the stops, released the brakes and the Liberator slowly started to accelerate down the runway, the first aircraft to head into the grey sky waiting for them.

Major McCoy put his hand on the throttles to stop them accidentally closing, and started calling out the airspeeds. On reaching 110 knots, John pushed gently on the yoke to stop the fully laden bomber taking off just above stalling speed, then when he had 130 knots and a safe margin, he pulled back on the control column and the bomber raised her nose and, a few seconds later, the wheels skipped a couple of times on the black asphalt of Runway 21, the Liberator took to the air and Don McCoy raised the undercarriage for a positive climb. Behind him Captain Web Uebelhoer in *Bad Penny* was already half way down the runway and 2nd Lt Edward Hautman in *Mairzy Doats* was just starting his take-off run, so three aircraft were using the 021 line of asphalt at the same time.

The occupants of Long Row farm, just off the end of the runway, were woken and the whole house shook as the bombers passed less than 100ft overhead. As the speed passed 135 knots, the flaps were raised and the Liberators started a turn to port to take up a northerly heading for Buncher 6 beacon, near Hethel, about five miles north of Tibenham. Stationed at Hethel was another group of the 2nd combat wing – the 389th – who were also going to bomb Kassel that day. The Tibenham aircraft then started to orbit and climb around the beacon, turning 90 degrees every five minutes to make a 'race track' pattern.

Back on Tibenham base, aircraft followed at 30-second intervals, with 2nd Lt Ed Hautman, in *Mairzy Doats*, taking off at 06:01. The procession continued until Lt Palmer Bruland in *Texas Rose* became the 38th and last to get airborne at around 06:25.

Forming up was a dangerous manoeuvre with hundreds of bombers circling their different 'Buncher' stations and airfields only on average five miles apart. They were also frequently handicapped by poor English weather and collisions were numerous. A few weeks earlier, over Tivetshall railway station, a mile from Tibenham airfield (where crews would catch the train to Norwich or London), two bombers had collided,

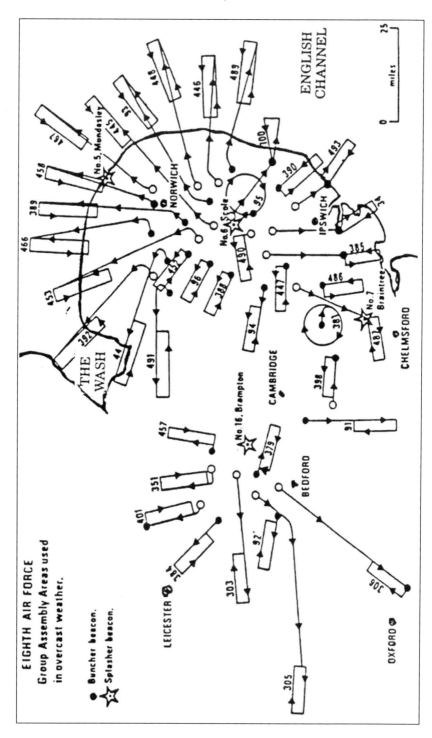

Race track patterns for the group formations. (Norfolk Gliding Club archive)

scattering wreckage and bodies over the junction. The railway station sported a new patch of slate roof where the body of a navigator had plunged through it, and at the nearby coal yard witnesses were horrified as the decapitated head of a crew member rolled across the yard like a bowling ball.

The group formatted on Chilton's aircraft as they flew the 'race-track' pattern around Buncher 6 beacon. Web Uebelhoer tucked in close to the starboard wing of Chilton's aircraft and could see Major McCoy sitting in the P2 co-pilot's right-hand seat. Lt William Hunter, in *Terrible Terry's Terror*, did the same, close to Chilton's port wing. As the next row formed up, Lt James Baynham in *King Kong* slid into the extreme starboard position, with the others following suit to get to their assigned positions. The process took until 07:55.

With Captain Chilton in the lead of 703 Squadron, 700 squadron formed up around him to lead the formation, with 702 squadron forming the high right, 701 the high high right and 703 the low left station. Then the group set off at an altitude of 12,000ft heading for the North Norfolk coast, crossing over the distinctive red-and-white lighthouse at Happisburg, south of Splasher 6 beacon at Mundesley at 8.03 am and heading due north to join the 389th and 453rd bomber groups about ten miles offshore to form the 2nd Combat Bomber Wing.

En route

At 08:14 the assembled wing of 315 Liberators of the division turned onto a heading of 116 degrees and started the long climb to 23,000 feet. Before the crew went on oxygen at 10,000 feet, the bombardiers struggled in their heavy, cumbersome flying clothing while they balanced on the narrow catwalk above the bomb bay doors to arm the bombs. The bomb-arming device was a small propeller secured by a safety pin and a wire connected to the bomb rack. The bombardier made sure the arming wires were still in place and took the cotter pins out, but he kept them safe in case he had to put them back for a full bomb-load landing. When the bombs were dropped, the end of the wires secured to the rack would pull the safety pin out. This allowed the propellers on the nose of the bomb to turn in the airflow and, after many rotations, this armed the bombs to explode on impact, or the delayed fuse would activate.

Climbing through the overcast sky and breaking out of the stratus cloud into the clear blue sky above, gunners tested their guns and crews donned their flak jackets and tin helmets as the enemy coast approached. Wearing their 'walk round' oxygen bottles the flight engineers/gunners climbed down from their top turrets and went to the bomb bay to transfer fuel from the auxiliary wing fuel cells to the main tanks.

As the group slowly gained altitude, problems associated with high altitude could occur. If a crewman accidentally unplugged himself from the plane's oxygen system and the problem went unnoticed, he would first get dizzy, then pass out. If oxygen was not restored quickly, he could easily die from anoxia. But the worst problem for crewmen in the waist position was not fear of losing oxygen, it was frostbite. Waist windows on the Liberator were open to a 200mph, minus forty degree slipstream. Exposure to this extremely cold air for even a few seconds could cause mild frostbite. So removing thick sheepskin gauntlets to clear a jam was a risky business, and contact between bare skin and metal would result in the skin sticking to the metal and being left behind when leaving go of the metal. Frequently fingers, toes and noses would be damaged by equipment failures or carelessness, getting the unfortunate crewman 'nipped'.

Aircrew had to be careful not to sweat because the sweat would freeze once higher altitudes were reached, making their task even more miserable. The cold would also cause ice to form in the oxygen masks. This had to be cleared frequently, by squeezing the tubes and mask to break up the ice, as it would block oxygen flow if left unchecked, with the inevitable results of unconsciousness and even death if not spotted in time.

All three of the airborne aborts came from the 701st Squadron in the high high right position. On route to the Dutch coast Lt Frost in *Slossie* had an ill crew member and turned back towards Tibenham, thus saving nine lives, the remaining thirty-seven continuing to climb, heading for landfall on the Dutch coast about twenty miles north of Amsterdam. Lt Wilkins in 701 squadron's *Heavenly Body* also experienced problems. He crash-landed on the continent, the aircraft languishing there until January 1945 when she was salvaged and returned to Tibenham. So Lt Wilkins avoided the catastrophe that was going to happen on this occasion. But it was only to delay his appointment with the 'Grim Reaper' as he was killed a few weeks later flying as co-pilot with another crew.

A formation of B24 Liberators from the 445th BG. This picture was taken on 6 October 1944, nine days after the Kassel mission. (NARA)

The first battle casualty occurred at 08:35. While climbing through 19,000ft, Lt McClelland in *Tahelenbak* lost an engine, aborted and returned to Tibenham, leaving thirty-five bombers to carry on towards the target. McClelland had a very disappointed crew as they had gone through all the stress but weren't going to get a mission credit for it.

Above cloud and at the briefed altitude of 23,000ft, the wing threaded its way across Holland and entered German airspace, avoiding the heavy flak around Munster, and trying to keep the Germans guessing what the target was. At 09:17, north-east of Münster, they turned south and headed for the initial point (IP). This was the designated spot where they would turn onto the bomb run. The 2nd Air Division arrived at the IP at 09:29, turned eastwards onto a course of 77 degrees and headed for Kassel. Bombardiers began synchronizing the Norden bombsight and the code name 'Pea Soup' was transmitted, meaning this was going to be a bombing through overcast (BTO) mission. The group would bomb when the lead bombardier in the PFF (pathfinder) ship dropped, and the rest of the group would 'toggle' theirs.

In the lead ship Major McCoy handed over control to one of the three lead navigators he had on board. Chief navigator 1st Lt Raymond Ische was assisted by 2nd Lt Cloys Johnson sitting at his 'Mickey' H2X ground radar, and 2nd Lt Carlton Hudson, as the pilotage navigator, now had command of the group's course. As with lots of things run by committee, it was at this point things started to go wrong. Ray's 'Mickey' ground radar blind-bombing aid was giving trouble and, combined with unexpected winds, the group started to go off course.

The Battle Begins

Down on the ground below, on the airfields of Lukau, Finsterwalde and Walzow, the Germans had assembled three Storm Groups (*Sturmgruppen*) of interceptor fighters – Focke-Wulf Fw 190 A-8/R2s and R8s of IV.(Sturm)/JG3, II.(Sturm)/JG4 and II.(Sturm)/JG300, along with Messerschmitt Bf109Gs of I./JG300.

The German equivalent of the British 'Big Wing', the Storm groups were the idea of German fighter ace General Adolf Galland. They were manned by volunteer pilots trained to close to less than 100 metres before opening fire. From that range they could hardly miss with their 30mm cannons and machine guns and caused havoc against the Allied 'Heavies'.

Galland's answer to the increasing effectiveness of the bomber groups and the advent of long-range fighter escorts was the *Sturmbock* (battering ram) eight-ton flying 'tanks', which were especially configured to attack bomber formations. The Sturmbocks included heavily-armoured Focke-Wulf 190A-8/R2 and Fw 190A-8/R8. The R2s had their outboard 20mm cannon replaced by the 30mm MK 108 cannon. The R8s had the MK 108 30mm cannon outboard of the propeller arc and additional pilot protection consisting of an armoured oil cooler, cockpit area, bullet-proof windshields and, because of the now nearly double fuel consumption, drop tanks and an auxiliary fuel tank behind the pilot's seat. All this weight needed an uprated BMW 801 2,400 hp engine hauling it into the sky. They were clumsy aircraft and needed the protection of a group of Me Bf 109Es acting as top cover.

All this made approximately 120 enemy aircraft ready to pounce on the approaching American bomber stream. The German pilots waited until the 'scramble' command came through, when the radar controllers had decided where the bombers' target was and worked out the best intercept point.

Meanwhile, higher up in the B-24 of Lt Chilton's lead aircraft, mistakes were being made which would have dire consequences. Probably due to an unexpected 70-knot tailwind, the plane overshot the point to turn south-east onto the bomb run, despite warnings from the lead navigator of the following 453rd Group. Having turned late, they steered on a heading of 67 degrees, which slowly split the 445th from the other two groups. Navigators in the following ships noticed the error and broke radio silence. Reg Miner, as 702-squadron lead, also had three navigators on board and he called Chilton's aircraft to warn them they were off course. But he was told to stay tight and they were going to bomb as a group rather than in trail. Major McCoy had decided to stay on course and bomb Göttingen as a target of opportunity. With that decision, the fate of the 445th was sealed.

If the weather permitted a visual bomb run, at the IP the squadrons would normally form into a line or trail, giving a more concentrated bomb pattern. However, if the ground was obscured, the group would keep in the combat box formation and drop when the PFF ship did, giving a more widespread pattern but increasing the chances of some hits on the target.

The bomb run was initiated, bomb doors opened and the gunners started to dump out chaff. Chaff or 'window' was a bundle of aluminum strips

The 2nd Combat wing's Liberators bomb Kassel on 27 September 1944. (NARA)

with paper wrappers. The strips, always cut the same length, reflected back the signal from the radar controlling the anti-aircraft guns and hopefully spoiled its aim as the chaff descended. The pilots of the lead crews gave over control to the bomb-aimers who, with their Norden bombsights, could steer the aircraft through its autopilot. This also meant the bomb run had to be straight and level, and evasive action for flak or fighters couldn't be taken. But this wasn't a problem as the 445th was now well away from the flak of well-defended Kassel, which the other groups on the correct heading were experiencing.

All the aircraft waited for the lead bombardier, 1st Lt Parker Trefethen to drop, then the group would all 'toggle' at the same time. At 09:41 the bombs were dropped, but they landed short of Göttingen, near the village of Grone, with little effect – the only known casualties being two cows.

Glad to be rid of the 6000lb load, the Liberators jumped skyward, needing some forward push on the control yokes and retrimming to maintain 23,000ft. The crews were also glad it was now time to head home, and the first of what was supposed to be two turns to the right was initiated. In fact it turned out to be one long continuous turn onto a heading of 152 degrees for the rendezvous point. The higher the bombers flew, the smaller the difference between the maximum (VNE) and stalling speeds became, which is why this part of the flight envelope was called 'coffin corner'. The ships on the inside radius of a turn had to slow down to hold position, and they sometimes came very close to a stall. When the aircraft was approaching a stall the controls would become loose and require a larger movement for the same effect as at a higher speed; the aircraft would start to mush, shudder and vibrate, and if allowed to stall would probably drop a wing – meaning the aircraft would start to roll towards the wing that was no longer providing lift. If the pilot didn't immediately push forward on the control yoke to un-stall the wings, the wing drop could develop into a full-blown spin; this was difficult to get out of and would lose thousands of feet in altitude for a big heavy aircraft like the B-24.

As the low left, squadron 703 had the greatest radius to travel and struggled to maintain position, spreading out in the process. It was still trying to reformate, when the first wave of approximately ten Fw190s came in to attack from the rear.

The German fighter pilots' main tactics, now the B-24 ball turrets had been removed, was to rake the fuselage from the rear and slightly below with their 20- and 30-mm cannons. This kept them out of the top and waist-gunner's sights and, having reduced the return fire from the Liberators by killing or wounding the waist and tail gunners, the German fighter pilots would usually concentrate fire on the wings, knowing they could easily set the fuel tanks alight.

At 10:03 the first attacks came in and within a couple of minutes all hell broke loose on the 445th outfit. First Lt Cecil Isom, flying *Patty Girl* and leading 703 squadron in the low low left position, heard from his tail gunner, S/Sgt Ray Phillips, that fighters were closing in from the six o'clock position and about the same altitude. Art Shay, who was sitting in the nose turret as pilotage navigator, thought this was the P47 escort turning up, but when the ship started shaking as Phillips began firing his twin 50-calibre machine guns, quickly joined by the waist- and top-turret guns, he realized they were under attack. Explosions of 20 and 30-mm cannon shells began bursting in orange and white all around as up to five Fw190s closed in line-abreast formation. White flashes from the leading edges indicated they were firing, and within moments *Patty Girl* was surrounded by burning Liberators. With Isom and co-pilot Lonnie Justus swinging violently to avoid burning aircraft, the first wave of Fw190s tore into the squadron. This gave Art a chance to fire at several as they went past, but they were followed by another wave close on their heels. Seeing that the Libs hadn't got belly turrets, some of the German fighter pilots attempted to attack from below. One Fw190 pulled up in a climbing turn just fifty yards from Art's turret, giving him a chance to rake him. Spouting black smoke and flames the enemy plane fell away. Now the Me109s and more Fw190s joined in the attack.

At the controls of his Focke-Wulf 190 A8, Red 19, Pilot Ernst Schroeder, was climbing hard along with the rest of the 5th Squadron, out of their base at Finsterwalde. As the thirty aircraft headed west, they reached 25,000 feet before the squadron caught up with the rear of the ensuing battle and scythed through the American bombers, some of which were already burning and exploding. Lining up his new type of gyro gunsight, Ernst quickly dispatched one Liberator before finishing off another which was already heavily damaged and on fire. Keen to confirm his victories Ernst pulled his Fw190 into tight turns, trying to avoid the falling wreckage and the many parachutes of those who had managed to escape the burning Liberators as he descended to witness the area of the crash sites of his victims. While trying to locate the location of the columns of smoke rising from funeral pyres of the B-24s Ernst was suddenly attacked by a 391st Fighter Group P51 Mustang and a dogfight ensued. Ernst's fighter took some 30-calibre rounds in the tail and he ran out of ammunition early in the engagement, having used most of it on the bombers earlier. So, a few minutes later, the German fighter pilot had to use all his skill to avoid the destructive firepower of the six 50mm Browning machine guns of a yellow-chequered-nosed Mustang, this time from the 353rd Fighter Group. After several passes he managed to escape by flying at extremely low level back to the nearest base at Langensalza, where a grateful German managed to land safely.

In 1985 Ernst Schroeder recounted some the events of his combat in a letter to the German historian Walter Hassenpflug.

On the 27th of Sept. 1944, the 2nd fighter squadron 300 with their Focke-Wulf 190 fighters was stationed at Finsterwalde airbase. It was only a temporary transfer, because we were really lying in Erfurt-Bindersleben.

Our group took off at 10 A.M. for an enemy engagement against a bomber air raid consisting of perhaps 30 airplanes. We had, according to my memory, an overcast sky and had to climb through a relatively thin cloud layer at about 1500-2000 meters altitude in order to get to the altitude of the in-flying Americans, who usually were lying at approximately 7500-8000 metres. By radio we were led to the in-flying bomber group by the so-called Y-command of the fighter division. Because we were flying over the clouds, we could not see the ground. The orders often changed our course direction, and we also never knew where we really were.

On our maps we would have to look for locations which were radioed and which we all heard in our headsets, but a pilot of a single-seater could not do that, because he had to concentrate on the flight of the group and the steering of the plane.

I remember that towards 11 A.M. we were radioed farther and farther west, that is, after at first flying back and forth it then went steady at about 270 degrees – therefore to the West. The commanding fighter officer speaking to us from the ground became more and more agitated and said we now had to see the enemy planes in front of us. Indeed we did.

After a short time, a large group of B-24 'Liberator' bombers flew like a swarm of mosquitoes right in front of us in the same course direction.

The fine silhouettes very soon became bigger and bigger because of our great speed. They were flying almost exactly at our altitude. But then suddenly several of these big ships began to burn and to plunge down with fire and smoke – even before we had given off a single shot, a fighter unit flying ahead of us had begun the attack.

Immediately the sky was full of parachutes and wreckage, and there we were flying right into it. My squadron captain and I had voluntarily installed for trial under engagement conditions a new aiming device as it was then called. We had gotten a gadget built into our airplanes.

Very rapid running, electrically driven gyros automatically calculated the necessary aiming allowances. Therefore one could shoot rather precisely and effectively from a greater distance than otherwise.

We were supposed to use that now. Well, the result was impressive in my case.

Even before I had covered the remaining distance to my bomber, it already stood in flame from the expended fire power of my six machine guns, that is, both left engines of the 'giant crate' were burning. The airplane turned on its side and plunged. Also the neighboring machine was already smoking from a previous attack. I only needed to change aim, to shoot again, and also this big enemy plane stood in bright flames. This new aiming gadget was functioning truly astonishingly.

I was so surprised and fascinated that I suddenly flew alongside my victim and stared at the meter-high flames which were pouring out of the hideous, bomb-filled, thick fuselage of this 'Liberator' all the way back beyond the elevator. Then the great crate clumsily laid itself over on its back and went down. All of this happened much faster than you can read it here!

In view of this surprising success, I naturally wanted to know precisely where my two opponents would fall, because a double shoot-down of two four-engine bombers (they were also my only ones) was already in 1944 for us something exceptional. The acknowledgement of the air victories was very much more probable with a detailed report.

Therefore, I circled the crashing wreckage of 'my' two adversaries in large downward running spirals. But my intention was hindered in the most horrible way, because the entire sky was full of parachutes with fliers who had jumped and also small and giant-sized airplane debris which suddenly cropped up in front of my windshield and which flew by me because of my high diving speed (600-700 km/h). I truly had to close my eyes often, because I believed with certainty I would have to ram something! It was simply disgusting!

Under me came the cloud layer through which here and there the surface of the Earth was quickly shimmering closer and closer. And through this cloud cover rose 10-15 columns of smoke from the explosions of the airplanes that in the meantime had already crashed. Since I could not estimate how high the clouds were above the ground, I had to fly though them in a flatter angle than I had been diving in until then, in order to avoid an eventual collision with the surface of the Earth myself. The wreckage of my two bombers had naturally crashed already through them with giant explosions. I flew through the relatively thin cloud layer, which now spread itself out at an altitude of about 7000 metres above the ground.

(This part of Ernst Schroeder's letter is reproduced by kind permission of the Kassel Mission Historical Society)

Tucked in just under Isom's port wing, co-pilot of the Mercer crew in ship 549, Leo Pouliot, maintained tight formation using manual control of the throttles as the auto function was u/s. When he saw Isom's tail-gunner, Phillips, start firing and white puffs of explosions started appearing throughout the formation, he realized they had been jumped by enemy fighters and switched to the escort fighter channel to cry for help. He got an immediate reply asking for their position and was just asking navigator Milton exactly where they were when all hell broke loose. The aircraft took several hits, one of which knocked out the radio.

The 701st Squadron boasted two Texas Roses, 2nd Lt Palmer Bruland's *Texas Rose* and Lt Paul Swofford's *Sweetest Rose of Texas*, but only one was going to survive that day. Palmer in *Texas Rose* was flying for the first time with this crew.

Palmer Bruland was born in Nebraska in 1921 to Peter and Marie Bruland, immigrants from Norway. They lived in a community of Norwegians and

Focke-Wulf 190 A8 Red 19, Pilot Ernst Schroeder. (Courtesy kasselmission.org via Linda Dewey)

he spoke Norwegian as a child. His father owned a large farm and worked the land growing wheat. Like a chapter from Steinbeck's *Grapes of Wrath*, in the Great Depression and 'dust bowl' era he lost the farm. The family of six drove out west in their car to settle in Seattle in a small house where they raised chickens. The war put a stop to Palmer's education and, after graduating from High School in 1939, he now sat in the left-hand seat in command of *Texas Rose*. But he could only watch through the Plexiglass cockpit windows as the first wave of German fighters tore through the 445th.

Palmer's co-pilot, Lt Peter Belitsos, was at the controls when their No.3 engine suddenly burst into flames. Palmer took over control, leaving a bewildered Belitsos to get his act together, cut the fuel supply and feather the prop on No.3 of the badly damaged *Texas Rose*. As the fire in the engine would not go out, Belitsos recalled, 'We flew for quite a while losing altitude and were now fully expecting that the ship would blow up, when Palmer hit the bail-out bell.' (kasselmission.org)

Bruland Crew. Back row, L to R: S/Sgt Stephen Gray, Eng. PoW; 2nd Lt Palmer M. Bruland, Pilot, PoW; unknown; unknown, PoW. Front row: 2nd Lt Norman J. Cuddy, Nav., PoW, believed to be on left. Others on crew but not pictured include S/Sgt Lee Huffman, waist gunner, and S/Sgt Ferdinand Flach, nose gunner, both of whom were murdered after they parachuted down safely and were captured; T/Sgt James H. Boman, radio operator, PoW; S/Sgt Hugh J. Sullivan, waist gunner, PoW; S/Sgt Charles M. Dove, tail gunner, PoW. Also not pictured is co-pilot Peter Belitsos. (Courtesy of KMHS)

Navigator 2nd Lt Norman J. Cuddy released S/Sgt Ferdinand K. Flach from the nose turret and the gunner bailed out from the bomb bay. Cuddy went through the nose wheel doors. Radio operator S/Sgt Stephen J. Gray and engineer T/Sgt James H. Boman followed them. As the autopilot was not working, pilot Palmer Bruland tried to trim the plane so he could get to the bomb bay and jump, but each time he let go of the controls and got out of his seat to leave, the ship rolled and he had to go back to his seat and regain control. This happened a few times before he finally made it out.

On the starboard side of the high high right squadron, opposite the Liberators of Bruland and Swofford, 1st Lt Edgar Walther and the crew of *Big Jane* took multiple hits from an attacking Fw190, the pilot of which, either by incapacity, bad judgement, or putting into practice the ramming oath he had taken, collided with the tailplane of the Liberator. The bomber immediately lost control and entered a spin, descending a few thousand feet before exploding and disintegrating in a fireball. 1st Lt Edgar Walther was the only survivor.

703 Squadron took heavy punishment in the first wave of attacks, with the ships of Elder in *Clay Pidgeon,* Mowat in *Hot Rock,* Johnson in *Fridget Bridget*, Fromm and Bolin all shot down. In a few short moments the sky was filled with burning aircraft struggling to stay airborne, wreckage and – for the luckier ones – parachutes. Some crew-members bailed out but pulled their rip cords too early and their chutes either hung up or caught fire. Others who were blown or fell out of exploding aircraft without their chutes clutched at the sky as if to grab some divine hand to stop their fall. It would take more than two minutes to fall from 20,000ft, so they had plenty of time to say their final prayers, mixed with curses and cries to Mother.

Second Lt Vergos was hit by cannon fire in the nose turret of *Clay Pidgeon*, leaving the turret jammed and him mortally wounded inside it. Despite the efforts of some of the crew to release him, six members of the crew managed to bail out before the stricken B-24 blew up, with 1st Lt Oliver Elder still in the left-hand pilot's seat. S/Sgt Gunner John Durr

Lt Oliver Elder's mount *Clay Pidgeon* went down a mile south of Lindernau. (Norfolk Gliding Club archive)

landed with a broken leg and was taken by horse and cart to the village for first aid. But the radio operator, T/Sgt John Donahue, wasn't to get the same treatment when he landed and wouldn't make it to a PoW camp, as the five other survivors did.

Lt Johnson's *Fridget Bridget* was no longer the immaculate, nearly-new aircraft he had boarded four hours earlier. Having had No.3 engine blown off, and then nose-wheel doors blown away – taking navigator Lt Bateman with them to his death – with the wing on fire Joe Johnson pressed the bail-out bell and all the remaining crew managed to bail out and get down safely. Bombardier 1st Lt James Dowling was knocked out on landing, captured and survived hostile locals throwing rocks, to be thrown into a local jail. Local kids came and stared at the bloody *Terrorflieger* through the cell window and ran away as soon as James made any movement.

The gallant crew was to suffer one more casualty before the killing had finished, as Navigator 2nd Lt William Flickner was to find out.

Out on the extreme port side of the low left squadron, Lt Andrew Seeds in the borrowed 702 Squadron aircraft *Steady Hedy* had both wings catch fire and then the aircraft blew up. Those inside stood no chance of getting out as the now wingless fuselage plummeted and tumbled to the earth 20,000 feet below, taking all the unfortunate crew to their deaths, trapped in their aluminium coffin.

First Lt Richard Fromm was flying at the back row of the squadron. His Liberator 080 took big hits in the early attacks from the Fw190s coming up from the rear and was soon on fire in both wings. Richard had no choice but to press the bail-out bell and, miraculously, all the crew were still unhurt by the onslaught of 20 and 30mm cannon fire. Crewmen in the front of the aircraft left through the nose-wheel doors, and navigator 1st Lt Charles McCann and S/Sgt Raymond Bence jumped from the nose turret. Radio operator T/Sgt Joseph Rackis followed them, and back in the fuselage the waist-gunners S/Sgt William Brower and S/Sgt Joseph Williams got out along with tail-gunner S/Sgt Lee Coffin. Tragedy then struck as co-pilot 2nd Lt Edward Globis was making his way rearwards, possibly to check all the gunners had got out OK. He was hit by an exploding cannon shell and became the only fatality from the crew. Richard Fromm and engineer T/Sgt Russell Lene were the last to leave as the aircraft veered away from *Hot Rock* flying on the port side and dropped away.

Technical/Sgt Theodore Myers, the engineer/gunner in 1st Lt William Mowat's *Hot Rock*, had fired his top turret guns until they kept jamming with the heat. When a cannon shell exploded nearby filling the turret with

Lt William Mowat's aircraft *Hot Rock*. (Norfolk Gliding Club archive)

smoke and bending one of his guns he decided enough was enough. But as he climbed down from the turret he saw streams of gasoline pouring into the bomb bay. He tried unsuccessfully to plug the leaks and got drenched in the gas, so he opened the bomb-bay doors to vent the fuselage, and then headed back to report the situation to William Mowat. On the way a 20-mm shell exploded by his feet wounding his right foot and both legs and knocking him onto his back on the catwalk. Moments later there was a blinding flash and he was set on fire and lost consciousness. When Theo came to he was hanging in his parachute, badly burned around the face, but at least the slipstream had put out the fire.

Theo and tail-gunner S/Sgt Frank Plesa, who was also badly burned, were the only survivors of the exploding *Hot Rock*. The rear turret, complete with Frank, was blown off when the Liberator exploded. Fortunately the tail-gunner was wearing a back-pack parachute and he managed to extricate himself from the tumbling turret and deploy his chute with his badly burnt hand. On the ground he was quickly captured by a Hitler youth sporting an old pistol, and the wounded and burnt Frank was assisted to a cottage where he was given first aid. He was then transported by horse and cart to the railway station and eventually wound up in Frankfurt hospital for several days, being treated by Catholic nuns.

Back up in the sky the German fighters weren't having it all their own way. With just Isom and Mercer still flying in the low low left position, it was down to the gunners of both aircraft to stop the rout from becoming total. A German fighter trying to exploit the lack of ball turret pulled up underneath Isom's belly with his Fw190 'prop hanging' and on the verge of stalling when he was hit by the twin 50s of Ted Hoiten in the nose turret of Mercer's aircraft. His fighter burst into flames, turned over on its back and disappeared in an inverted spin. Hoiten's action saved *Patty Girl* and the Isom crew.

Another Fw190 attacked Mercer's bare-aluminium Liberator from the two o'clock position but exploded in a cloud of debris when he was raked with fire from the twin 50-calibre guns of Kenneth Kribs in the top turret. But another German fighter attacked immediately from the eight o'clock position and inflicted some serious damage when he shot off one of the rudders, hit the hydraulic reservoir and oxygen bottles and damaged the control lines. This left the Liberator of Lt Mercer badly damaged. Over in the nose turret of Isom's ship, Art Shay watched as Cecil Isom swung left to avoid the burning Liberator on their right. Just in front of him another bomber disintegrated, with two props spinning off into space. Now Me109s were scything through the formation. But Ken Kribs, still in the top turret of Lt Mercer's ship, got a bead on an Fw190 pulling up in a climbing turn in front of him, and raked him with bullets until black smoke and orange flames appeared. The two 703 Squadron Liberators mutually safeguarded each other throughout the attack.

Things weren't going well for the other squadrons either. Reg Miner, regarded as one of the best pilots in the group, quite often had to take 'rookie' pilots on missions as co-pilot. It was the custom for new crews to have their pilot doing a mission with an experienced pilot before being let loose to fly with their own crew. Reg was on his 20th mission flying in the lead of 702 Squadron. In the high right position, he had just completed his final turn back into formation when the ship was hit from the rear. Rear gunner S/Sgt Arthur Lamberson didn't get a shot off before the incoming cannon fire cut all the hydraulic lines and put his turret out of action. The autopilot was put out and the aircraft reared up, but Reg quickly disconnected the autopilot and pushed the yoke forward to regain control, only for the aircraft to be hit again by four Fw190s lined up and concentrating fire on the already partly-disabled Liberator. Radio operator Joe Gilfoil yelled, 'there's a fire in the bomb bay,' and top-turret gunner Mac Thornton was blown out of his turret with his face slashed by shards of Plexiglass and streaming with blood, which rapidly froze in the minus 28 degree air. Joe Gilfoil was mortally wounded when another cannon shell almost took his leg off, leaving it hanging by a thread of skin. One of the waist-gunners, Alvin Kitchens, was hit in the backside.

Gasoline poured into the bomb bay from the ruptured tanks, but ventilation caused by all the holes and the lack of top turret prevented a build-up of fumes and an inevitable explosion. Up in the nose, gunner Charlie Jackson was still firing at the fighters as they came close and Reg and co-pilot Virgil Chima struggled to keep the stricken aircraft flying. But when they looked out to see both wings on fire at the wing tank fillers, they realized it was time to get out. Reg pressed the bail-out button, Virgil looked at him and Reg told him to go. In the back the gunners put a chute on Joe Gilfoil and threw him out, hoping the freezing air would stem the blood flow. Then they followed him. The 'mickey' radar operator, Branch Henard, had accidentally deployed his parachute, so he had to bail out holding it gathered up in his arms. Fortunately for him it worked.

The normal way out for most of the crew was through the bomb bay doors, but they were damaged and jammed. Navigator Frank Bertram kicked frantically at the frozen nose-wheel doors, which suddenly gave way leaving him dangling with one leg hanging out. He pulled himself back in and, sitting on the edge, looked back to see the rest of the crew behind him ready to go and pointing to him to get out. So he dropped out feet first into the void, closely followed by the others, leaving Reg alone in the aircraft. He struggled to disconnect his oxygen mask, intercom and flak jacket while keeping control of the aircraft and, looking back, he saw the bomb bay doors were still firmly shut, so he went out through the open nose-wheel doors. The spinning aircraft dropped to 10,000 feet before he finally managed to extricate himself, only to find himself trapped under the wing and not wanting to deploy his chute in case it fouled on something. He fought to clear himself and, finally pushing himself clear of the aluminium ceiling of the wing, pulled the rip cord. A few seconds later he hit the ground, only 100ft from the burning wreck of the Liberator.

Second Lt Eugene George, co-pilot of the Brent crew in *Eileen*, knew they were off-course and without fighter escort. There were frantic calls on the radio to summon help from the fighters and Eugene heard tail-gunner S/Sgt Woodard Watts call that there were fighters approaching from the rear. The co-pilot replied, 'That's great,' only to be told by Woodrow, 'They're not ours.' Eugene soon realised they were under attack. *Eileen*'s guns were firing and the sound was almost like rain as shells and shrapnel

Reg Miner and crew. (Norfolk Gliding Club archive)

hit the olive-drab-painted aluminium of her wings and fuselage. Out on the extreme right of 702 Squadron, Eugene was concentrating on keeping the aircraft in formation, with his port wing tucked in with 1st Lt James Baynham's *King Kong*. Eugene was aware his plane had been badly hit and, with the No.2 engine on fire just outside his window, he pushed the bail-out button in the hope of giving the crew enough time to get out alive.

But he couldn't contact the front and rear sections of the crippled Liberator on the intercom, so Eugene left his right-hand seat and headed back down the fuselage. In the cockpit area, the radio operator, engineer, and top-turret gunner were supposed to leave through the bomb bay doors on the sound of the bail-out bell while the pilots concentrated on flying the airplane until they got clear. When he saw top-turret gunner New Yorker T/Sgt Constant Galuszewski and radio operator T/Sgt Sammy Weiner, from the Los Angeles area, still in their positions, Eugene had to crawl up there and tug the gunner down from his turret by the seat of his pants. Sammy Weiner didn't have his parachute harness on. Still under attack from a German fighter who was turning and doing 'split-S' aerobatics to keep firing at *Eileen*, Eugene got Weiner's harness and shoved it at him, opened the door into the bomb bay, and was confronted with a wall of flame.

The bomb bay doors were still closed and he had to operate a hydraulic switch to open them. But this was between the fuel gauges which were now on fire. There were fires all over the bomb bay with areas of flame chasing up pipes and pipework. As he went for the switch to open the doors, Eugene could only hope *Eileen* still had hydraulic power because there was no chance of standing in the flames long enough to wind the doors open by hand. So he jumped through the flames on the catwalk and hit the switch. Fortunately the bomb-bay doors opened. Returning through the flames, Eugene found Galuszewski standing there in a daze. He snapped the chest-pack parachute harness on him and got Weiner into his. When the pilot, 1st Lt Donald Brent, came past them into the burning bomb bay and bailed out, the three of them followed – and survived the jump.

B-24 H #42-50324 *Eileen* eventually crashed 2km south of Ulfen. Of the nine crewmen on board, three bailed out and survived: Eugene George, Constant Galuszewski, and Sammy Weiner. Four bailed out but didn't survive. First Lt Donald Brent (pilot) landed on the road between Grandenborn and Netra where he was immediately shot by Policeman Georg Schultheiss. The gunners in the rear of the plane, S/Sgt Woodard Watts (tail-gunner), S/Sgt Milton Smisek (waist-gunner), and S/Sgt George Linkletter (waist-gunner), all bailed out but didn't survive. Possibly some or all might have fallen into the hands of hostile civilians. There is no information on their fate. Sammy Weiner, having delayed opening his parachute, landed safely and saw another chute landing close by, so he headed off in that direction to meet up with its occupant, only to bump into a couple of German farmers who took him to a farmhouse. After a while he was marched at gunpoint to the nearby wreckage of *Eileen,* which still contained the bodies of two of his crew. The two remaining crewmen, 2nd Lt Harold Mercier (navigator) and S/Sgt Donald Larsen (nose-gunner), hadn't bailed out and their bodies were later recovered from the aircraft wreckage. Both were believed to have been killed when a number of cannon shells from the German fighters struck the nose section of the aircraft.

Second Lt Leslie Warman, flying *Our Gal* at the rear of 702 squadron, struggled to maintain control as hit after hit made the aircraft shudder and No.3 engine burst into flames. Thick black smoke filled the fuselage but rear-gunner S/Sgt Raymond Ray wasn't going down without a fight. When an Fw190 pulled up so close he could literally see the whites of the pilot's eyes (as his goggles where pushed up) he blasted it with his twin 50-calibre machine guns and the Fw190 exploded in a flash of flame and disintegrating debris. Moments later a burst of incoming fire disabled his guns, knocked him over backwards, and the bomb bay burst into flames. He hit the switch to open the doors and Raymond rolled out.

Flight engineer S/Sgt Wilbur Brown and S/Sgt Francis Barnish, nose-turret gunner, bailed out through the nose-wheel hatch and the three of them were the only survivors as the crippled Liberator and the rest of the crew plummeted earthwards in their blazing coffin.

Just behind Reg Miner's lead aircraft, 2nd Lt Howard Jones was in serious trouble as waves of Fw190s had riddled the fuselage of *Roughhouse Kate,* wounding the waist- and top-turret gunners and turning the tail turret into a blazing inferno. Tail-gunner S/Sgt Ray Paulus emerged from the turret covered in burning hydraulic fluid. He collapsed in a smoldering heap on the fuselage floor to die in the aircraft along with the mortally-wounded flight engineer/top-turret gunner T/Sgt Andrew Fratta who had been hit in the head. The rest of the crew managed to escape the blazing aircraft, but for co-pilot 2nd Lt Howard Allen a nasty reception committee was waiting for him on the ground.

702 Squadron 2Lt Leslie Warman's *Our Gal.* (NARA)

Among the German pilots causing havoc was Lt Oskar Romm of IV. (Sturm)/JG 3. Romms' victims that day were B-24s of the 445th BG. The three Liberators which went down in flames to his attacks were his 81st to 83rd victories. He later wrote, 'This mission was carried out in the classic Sturm battle group with the other Sturmgruppen. Hptm Wilhelm Moritz was at the head of our Angriffskeil or arrowhead formation. As leader of 15 Staffel, I attacked an element of B-24 Liberators. As had been the case over Oschersleben on 7 July our tactics were the same – a salvo into the fuselage and rear gunner's compartment to nullify the bombers return fire and then to set the wing root area near the engines on fire with our cannon.' The following day Oskar Romm shot down two more bombers to claim his 84th and 85th victories.

While this was happening, the rest of 702 Squadron was being annihilated.

Out on the starboard edge, Lt Jim Baynham, flying his 11th mission in *King Kong*, was one of the first to come under attack. S/Sgt Ray Lemons, the married waist-gunner from Dallas, Texas, had wanted to be a P51 pilot and had enlisted with his two buddies, who both went on to become pilots, but he failed the medical with a leg problem. Ray was sent on a gunnery course and then shipped over on the *Queen Elizabeth*, listening to the Glenn Miller band most of the way (the famous musician and his band were also in transit to the European Theatre of Operations (ETO) and were using time on the trans-Atlantic journey to practice). Ray arrived at Tibenham on 14 June, but now, three months later, he stood at the Liberator's waist window clutching the right 50-calibre machine gun. Unlike most of the rest of the crew, the gunner was only on his eighth mission because the ball turret had been removed and there was a spare gunner in the Baynham crew. Rather than split the crew up, they alternated, with one of the gunners staying behind on each mission. On this disastrous flight the lucky guy was S/Sgt Lord, who was still safely in his cot at Tibenham, while Ray, freezing at 23,000 feet over Germany, watched as fighters approached from the rear.

The fighters attacked from behind and below and *Kong* was hit between engines one and two, leaving a nine-inch hole and blowing away the aileron on the port wing. T/Sgt Howard Boldt, blazing away in the top turret, fired more than 100 rounds from his twin 50s as the endless attacks came in. *King Kong's* bomb bay burst into flames and smoke immediately filled the cockpit. Howard dropped down from his turret to report to Jim Baynham that they were on fire and it was time to get out. In the nose in a gun turret sat Hector Scala, the bombardier. He had fought off a nose attack with his fifty calibre machine guns before he heard the alarm bell and headed for the bomb bay.

The crew managed to put out a fire in the generator and they opened the windows to clear the smoke. But attacks from both head-on and behind started more fires in the bomb bay. Jim told the crew to bail out. Ray Lemons and John Knox, the waist-gunners, were the first to go. They landed twenty miles from where the *Kong* eventually crashed. She had flown another seven or eight miles by the time the next to get out, Howard Boldt and James Fields, had put on their chutes, opened the hatch into the nose-wheel compartment and hit the auxiliary bomb-bay opening switch on the way. The doors partially opened, which cleared some of the smoke and flames but, as Howard was just preparing to jump, an exploding cannon shell put some two-inch pieces of shrapnel into his legs, breaking both of them. He fell through the open hatch, pulled his ripcord, which immediately opened his parachute with a tug, and watched the circling fighters as he lapsed into unconsciousness.

Hector Scala, James Fields and John Cowgill also made it down in one piece. But, as some of the crew were to discover, where you came down could have serious consequences for your chances of survival. With the crew gone, Jim Baynham was now alone in the aircraft. He tried to foil the German fighters by lowering the undercarriage. An Me109 formatted on his wing and for a few moments both pilots looked at one another. It was time for Jim to get out, so, with a short pause to do up his parachute leg straps, he bailed out. Free-falling clear of the raging air battle, he waited to fall through the clouds and only pulled his ripcord when he saw the ground getting closer. Most of the others had opened their chutes as soon as they left the aircraft and wound up in the middle of the battle, with burning aircraft all around. Waist-gunner Ray Lemons had a close call when the air in his chute was almost spilled by a fighter streaking past. It took several minutes to descend from 20,000ft and the falling airmen were blown miles downwind, causing the crew to be widely spread over the German countryside. In some cases this cost them their lives.

Howard Boldt landed in a tree. Despite having two broken legs he managed to climb down, but could go no further and lay there in the middle of a small forest where nothing stirred and it was quite peaceful. After a while a small German aircraft flew over the area searching for evaders, spotted his chute, which was still hanging in the tree, and after a few hours Howard heard a German soldier approaching. He raised his hands and shook his head as the German demanded to know whether he had a pistol.

He was surrounded by a group of six German soldiers, searched, and maybe it was because Howard had a German sounding name, blue eyes and fair hair they treated him well. They lit him a cigarette, offered him a shot of morphine from his emergency phials and, constructing a stretcher out of tree branches and his parachute, they carried him away to a hand cart, which was pushed to the nearest village.

Out on the extreme port side of the high right 702 squadron, 2nd Lt Herbert Potts, pilot of *Annie McFannie*, was hit and slumped, mortally wounded, over the controls. His co-pilot, 2nd Lt Gerald Kathol, ordered the bailout from the now blazing aircraft and, as the crew struggled to extricate themselves from the stricken aircraft, finding the bomb bay doors inoperable and the bomb bay a mass of flames from all the ruptured fuel lines, they were just trying to escape from the cockpit when *Annie* exploded and disintegrated, throwing only four survivors out of the doomed Liberator. On the other side of the squadron, 'Mac' MacGregor, who had been eating fresh eggs for breakfast five hours earlier with 'Doc' Cochran, co-pilot of 1st Lt John French's crew, and discussing the fact his last mission was going to be a 'milk run', now realized the error of his judgement. 'Doc' would be eating in France that evening, but it would be a long time before 'Mac' got another egg for breakfast.

Meanwhile, Ernst Schroeder's Focke-Wulf 190 Red 19 was pumping cannon shells into the stricken *Fort Worth Maid*. In line with the tactics of getting the gunners first, he concentrated his fire on the waist and rear sections of the B-24 and a SINGLE cannon shell decapitated both gunners, Sgts Bob Imhoff and Bill Stephens. T/Sgt William Stephens didn't like his assigned position in the top turret, he found it to cramped and claustrophobic, so he had swopped places with waist gunner S/Sgt Ammi Miller – a decision which cost him his life, as he was hit in the face by a cannon shell which killed him instantly.

First Lt Carl Sollien, a sign painter, artist and piano player, was, after twenty-five missions, an excellent pilot. He wasn't a 'throttle jockey' but used his aviation skills to keep in formation using less gas than other pilots by manipulating the supercharger settings to keep his aircraft in its place. But having extra fuel wasn't going to help him today, as he looked out so see his wing and engine on fire, then realised his control yoke wasn't connected to the elevators any more. He signalled that the crew should get out of the badly-damaged *Fort Worth Maid* as soon as possible. Not needing to set up his bombsight in the front turret, as they had bombed as a group,

Mac was still at the navigator's table behind the pilots, but he had left his parachute on the catwalk handy for the front turret. When he heard all the firing and shuddering as the B-24 took hits, Mac decided it would be a good idea to get it and jumped down to the entrance to the bomb bays to retrieve it. He was clipping it to the harness when an exploding cannon shell sprayed thirteen fragments of shrapnel into his legs. Looking at his friend and pilot Carl Sollien, whose expression was underlining the urgency of getting out of the now uncontrollable *Fort Worth Maid*, Mac hit the bomb bay door opening lever, but only the left door moved, and threw himself on the partly-open door, through which gasoline from the torn fuel lines was pouring, and rolled out into the icy blast of the air-flow. Navigator 2nd Lt Wes Huddleston, a smallish guy, was having trouble getting the nose-wheel doors to open and was jumping on them frantically, having caught his chute on something, he now carried a bundle of silk in his arms. But he still jumped through the doors and fortunately the parachute worked for him. Carl Sollien was about to bail out but the co-pilot, 2nd Lt William Koenig, was struggling with his parachute which had caught on something, so Carl gave him push to free the chute from the seat. A few moments later, as Carl stood up to get out, he had to step over the body of the co-pilot lying face down on the flight deck. He thought William had been shot and was dead – so Carl jumped. Second Lt John Dent for some reason didn't make it out and was later found dead still in the nose of the aircraft. Mac Macgregor recalled later: 'The nose turret guy [2Lt John Dent] was on his 5th mission and I thought this was kind of a funny thing. When we started the mission he said, "You guys don't have to worry. Nothing ever happens when I'm on a mission." Well, I thought he was a little bit scared and whether or not he froze, I don't think he was hit by a bullet, he was still in the nose of the plane when the pilot went back there. There was no evidence that he'd been shot or anything, he just never got out of the plane.'

About 100 feet away from the wreckage lay the body of co-pilot William Koenig, who was unwounded apart from a mark on his chin. It is most likely he had KO'd himself when he jumped and, recovering, had either bailed out too low for his chute to open or it had failed. S/Sgt Charles Graham, from Oklahoma, had managed to get out through the bomb bay. He was one of only five to survive out of the ten guys who had hauled their young bodies aboard *Forth Worth* that morning. It would be a long time before Carl's piano-playing fingers would 'tinkle the ivories' again.

Mac MacGregor hadn't waited very long before pulling his ripcord, so he was a long time in the descent and many miles downwind from the other survivors. The violent jerk of the chute opening had snapped the laces of his shoes tied to the harness and they, along with his flying boots, had fallen earthwards. So Mac joined the ranks of the many shoeless that day. He later remembered a feeling of complete loneliness as he drifted downwards and, seeing two Mustangs fly past, he could only wait and wonder on the reception he was about to receive from the waiting Germans. He landed heavily in a ploughed field and sprained his ankle, but was fortunate to be taken into custody by two Wehrmacht soldiers who arrived in a small car. They loaded Mac into the back seat and set of for a field where they were gathering the prisoners, saying the usual line 'for you the war is over'. And, for Mac, they were right.

With the exception of Krivik, flying a badly-damaged B-24 called *Percy*, 702 Squadron had ceased to exist. Along with Reg Miner and Jim Baynham, the crews of Potts, Schaen, Jones, Donald, Sollien, Warman and Brent had all been shot down and a trail of debris, empty chutes and bodies lay scattered across the German countryside. *Flossye*, *Fort Worth Maid*, *Annie McFannie* and *Rough House Kate* were now just burning wreckage – and in some cases coffins.

Up front, the leading elements weren't faring much better. Captain John Chilton and Major Don McCoy in the lead 703 Squadron aircraft were early casualties, closely followed by most of the 700 Squadron aircraft.

Inspecting the wreckage of Lt Sollien's *Fort Worth Maid*. (Courtesy of Mona MacGregor English)

The fields the other side of the road are the crash sites of:- left 2nd Lt Seed's *Steady Hedy*, centre Lt Sollien's *Fort Worth Maid* and on the right Lt Walther's *Big Jane*. (Author's collection)

The deputy lead crew of Web Uebelhoer tucked in close to the starboard wing of Chilton's aircraft and heard tail-gunner John Hubicz call that there were an awful lot of fighters behind them. Web thought it was the fighter escort playing about, but was soon disillusioned when exploding cannon shells started to appear around the aircraft. Then two Fw190s shot past, very close over both wings. One was hit by the twin 50mm machine guns in the nose turret and had one wheel descend and peel off damaged. Web could see Major McCoy sitting in the right-hand seat of Chilton's aircraft and watched helplessly as an Fw190 pulled up almost to the stall just 50ft below the aircraft and raked the whole fuselage of Chilton's ship with cannon fire.

Soon an orange glow appeared from the flames inside and Don McCoy signalled frantically at Web who, not knowing what he was trying to communicate, watched as Chilton lost control, rolled to the left and started down. He also saw some of the crew bail out. Inside Chilton's ship the gunners all managed to get out successfully before the lead ship exploded and broke in two, catapulting burnt navigator 2nd Lt Johnson Cloys out. He was the last survivor to escape as the plummeting front section of the fuselage took Captain John H. Chilton and three others to their deaths on the green fields below. Web took over as lead crew, not knowing a shell had passed through the oil reservoir on his No.2 engine, but the self-sealing rubber lining had done its job and the engine continued to run.

As the Fw190s sliced through 703 Squadron again, 2nd Lt Roy Bolin's ship 355K burst into flames from stem to stern, rolled over and plummeted earthwards, leaving the tail gunner Sgt Orland Schooley the only survivor.

Out on the port side in 1st Lt William Hunter's *Terrible Terry's Terror*, photographer-observer Sgt Tom Spera observed the horror going on around him. When he returned to Tibenham he wrote this graphic account: 'The leading Liberator, on fire from nose to tail, came swinging towards us like a severely wounded animal, then peeled away as if to pick a spot away from us to die. The next bomber moved up in its place. One Liberator with two engines on fire on the left wing came up from below us to explode when it reached our level. A human form fell out of the orange-coloured ball of fire. As he fell through space without parachute or harness, he reached up as if to grasp at something.'

Behind Web's now leading aircraft, there were only three aircraft left. Lt William Hunter in *Terrible Terry's Terror*, Lt French in *Asbestos Alice*,

A victim – believed to be the final moments of Lt Chilton's ship – goes down on the Kassel raid. (Norfolk Gliding Club archive)

On the right is Major Don McCoy, KIA 27 September flying in Captain John Chilton's lead ship. On the left is Major Howard Kreidler, 700 squadron commander, who survived the war and later became Brigadier General deputy director of operations, (J-3), US Strike Command. (NARA)

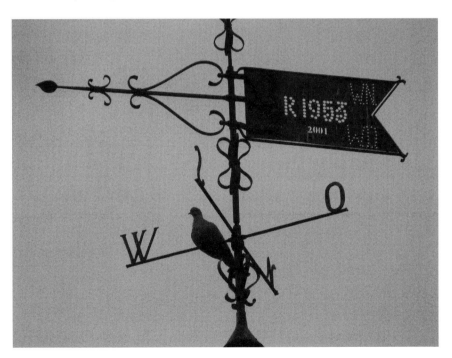

The weather vane that adorns the Church at Krauthausen, made from the wreckage of 2nd Lt Roy Bolin's aircraft. (Author's collection)

closely followed by Lt Heitz in *Bugs Bunny*, where tail-gunner S/Sgt Maynard Watson and waist-gunners Elroy Palm and Louis Ochevsky were engaged in a vicious fight with three Fw190s. Maynard, who had destroyed at least one and heavily damaged the others, was suddenly blown out of his turret when he was hit by several cannon shells under his feet. Thrown onto his back and engulfed in flames, he rolled over to smother the fire. Then he headed down the fuselage to find Elroy badly wounded and Louis Ochevsky mortally wounded on the cabin floor. He seized some burning dinghies and was throwing them out of the left waist window when he spotted an Fw190 only thirty feet away shooting cannon rounds into the wing of the crippled Liberator. He grabbed the idle waist 50-calibre machine gun and, sure he couldn't miss, blew the German pilot's head off.

The remaining Liberators continued in formation, but all of them had sustained heavy damage and they struggled to maintain what was left of the lead 700 Squadron formation. Raked by 30 and 20mm cannon fire, 2nd Lt Robert Hansen's *Hare Force* was in serious trouble. The plane was ablaze and, with some crew members wounded, only four managed to escape before the aircraft blew up with such violence the five remaining crew members on board were blown to pieces. Of the four who did get out, gunner S/Sgt Howell died of wounds, which left just three heading for a PoW camp.

The aircraft of Bruce, Hansen, Pearson, and Carrow, had been destroyed and fallen out of the sky.

Making up the numbers at the back of 700 Squadron was the 703rd aircraft of 2nd Lt Edward Hautman, on their 18th mission who, along with his co-pilot 2nd Lt Carroll Snidow, struggled to keep the battered *Mairzy Doats* aloft. An Fw190 had destroyed the tail turret and one rudder, fatally wounding S/Sgt Gordon Waldron. With No.4 engine 'running away' and the prop no longer able to be 'feathered' as it had lost oil pressure, it was only a couple of minutes before the prop tore itself and the engine from the wing, taking out No.3 engine in the process. Now down to two engines and with both pilots needed to push full rudder pedal down on what was left of their tail to keep the seriously-damaged *Mairzy Doats* flying straight, she fell away from what was left of 700 Squadron with two huge holes in the wing. The plane lost altitude rapidly and the crew threw everything they could find overboard and tried to head westwards towards France and safety. Fortunately, they were picked up by a couple of P38 Lightning fighters who escorted the still descending *Mairzy*, which was flying only just above stalling speed, and headed south-west for nearly forty minutes before their luck ran out and they were hit by flak near Koblenz. The end of the road had come and the crew bailed out. Pilot Edward Hautman was seen to bail out successfully only to be killed on landing. Along with the tail gunner and left waist-gunner S/Sgt John Tarbert, he became the third member of the crew to die that day. Carroll and the rest of the crew were soon captured and were told, 'For you the war is over.'

First Lt John French, from Massachusetts, who was on his 35th and last mission, was flying the nearly-new, shiny, unpainted aluminium *Asbestos Alice* in the upper right of the lead squadron. He had arrived in the UK in May flying a new bomber over the Northern route via Canada, Greenland and Iceland to Prestwick in Scotland. On arrival he was soon relieved of the new bomber and, after doing the usual familiarization courses in Northern Ireland, had been posted to Tibenham. French and his crew flew their first mission on D-Day. Due to the pressure of operations, crews flew many missions to Normandy in support of the Operation Overlord landings. These were mainly short flights – sometimes two or three a day – to coastal France on the 'No Ball' missions against the German V-weapon launch sites. This way crews quickly got through their required thirty missions, so the 'brass' raised the bar to thirty-five.

Only the guns of John's aircraft had kept the swarming German fighters off *Asbestos Alice*, which had lost the aircraft of Bruce and Hautman from either side. S/Sgt Herbert Schwartz knew their turn was coming, but Herbert in the tail-turret, and the two waist-gunners, fought a vicious battle to keep the marauding fighters away. Herbert scored many hits on them but, handicapped by his right gun jamming, an Fw190 came in close and did some serious damage. He takes up the account of the vicious fight:

> These fighters were coming in in groups of 15 and all ready for the kill – which was us! We were flying damn good formation and in a good position should we be hit by fighters. They looked to me to be attacking from north but I was wrong. Everyone started firing and before I knew it, they were in on us. One hundred Fockwulf's (*sic*) and I was half scared to death. They were thru us and started to reform for tail attack and I knew it was my job to hold them off. I pulled my flak suit off, threw my helmet off, and turned on my trigger switch and was ready for what may come. They headed for Bruce and Pearson, flying off our wings before they hit us in numbers. Everything started to run thru my mind. Pilot said to be careful

and take it easy. A FW came for me and I started shooting. Every attack but two were at 6:00 level and a dead-on shot. I let him have both guns and he started smoking and peeled beneath us. I looked up and saw Bruce's ship being attacked in formation by 7 fighters, and at the same time a fighter coming in at his waist. His guns were all firing away, and at that split second, another fighter came in at his topside of fuselage. He was on fire, and his plane got out of control. Another fighter started at his left waist and after throwing quite a bit of ammo, turned and headed for my tail, his engine already smoking. Fleming, left waist-gunner had hit him and now not knowing he was in trouble he came in on me. I let go and after firing about 30 rounds, he blew up at about 50 yards away from my turret. He had it, and Fleming and I were responsible for the kills. Lt Bruce was completely in flames, as I was later told by right waist-gunner. No chutes emerged and ship was out of control. His ship started towards us out of control, but French was on lookout for same. Another FW came in, I fired but he peeled off to our left. Before I go on, I want to say that my left waist-gunner scored 3 kills and my right waist gunner scored 1 kill. So these ships may have been downed by them on the peel off from the tail. I did not have time to keep watching them. Immediately following this another FW came in. I let loose both guns and I could have sworn I got him. We can take credit only for ships we see break up or completely on fire, or where pilot evacuates his ship. I had to hit him – he came in so close that I could have thrown a rock and hit him. I even believe I could have seen his facial expressions if I had had time to look. He peeled off and I guess the waist gunner made the kill. Planes coming at tail either peeled off to either side or under the ship. I now had time to get a second glance at Pearson off our right wing. I saw 2 chutes go out and all four of his engines were on fire. Now, our two wing lanes were down, and we were next to concentrate on. All this time, everyone was hollering on interphones and it was quite difficult to report all planes. Before I could look around, another 190 coming right for me. I started to fire both guns and after about 20 rounds my left gun stopped and right after this my right gun stopped. Here was this 190 coming at me and I had both guns out. I grabbed both charging cables. Charged my left gun and my right gun was not able to be charged. By this time he was on me and I got off about 10 rounds before he peeled off. This ship was the one that caused us all the trouble. My right guns failed to fully chamber the round, and a shell was stuck half in and half out of the chamber, making it impossible to charge. This 190 lodged a 20 millimetre in our No.4 tank, in our number 3 tank, blew off our right rudder, knocked out our No. 1 engine and made a 2 x 3 ft. hole in our flap and wing. Another few inches and we would have caught fire. We began to leak gas at a rate of 25 to 50 gallons a minute, and radioman said our bomb bay looked like Niagra (*sic*) Falls. We were crippled. We feathered No. 1 engine and our plane began to rock up and down. My tail turret was shaking back and forth (shaking the hell out of me – all due to rudder condition) and I had to leave here. I was hysterical and screamed over interphone to see what was wrong. I thought we were in a spin but co-pilot said we were all right and to take it easy. I laid a piece of flak suit on floor behind turret, and I fell to my knees to standby for other aircraft. My turret was out of control and only way I could operate her was under power, and this was still quite a job. Will to this day never understand why my tail turret never came off or why I wasn't killed. Will always be thankful for this moment.

(Courtesy of KMHS)

In the cockpit of *Asbestos Alice*, Lt John French, who had thought his last mission was going to be a 'milk run', was coming to the conclusion this was not going to be a normal day at the office. She was now perforated with holes, and shells had taken out the prop on No.1 engine, his instruments and the port rudder.

Second Lt William Bruce, pilot of the 700 Squadron aircraft *Bonnie Vee*, knew it was the end of the fight. Two weeks earlier he had managed to get the badly-damaged aircraft back to England after his co-pilot – also called William – had his left leg almost removed at the knee by an unexploded German 88 shell passing through the cockpit. Second Lt William Brown had put his right hand into his wounded leg, which was only hanging on with a little skin and tendon, to grasp the torn arteries and staunch the flow of blood, thus remaining conscious and stopping himself bleeding to death,

B-24J - 1 - FO T/N: 42-50784
700th BS RCS: D-Dog "Asbestos Alice"

Lt French crew's Liberator *Asbestos Alice*. (Courtesy Mike Simpson 445bg.org)

while calmly helping Bruce fly the crippled aircraft with his left hand. The *Bonnie Vee,* named after William Bruce's wife *Vyrlin*, had her port rudder and elevator totally destroyed, but the Williamses had managed between them to get her back down on an emergency field. Now with the new co-pilot, 1st Lt John Willet, the repaired *Bonnie Vee* was in serious trouble again. But this time fatally.

Out on the extreme starboard edge of the lead squadron, *Bonnie* had been badly hit several times and, with two engines on fire and nearly all the gunners killed or badly wounded, it was time to get out. The pilot rang the bail-out bell. William asked his new co-pilot, John Willet, to unbuckle his seat straps and, as John stood up, he was cut in half by a cannon shell. At that moment *Bonnie* was rammed by a Fw190, which tore away part of the right wing and tail, and went into a spin. The left wing exploded, leaving just a disintegrating fuselage tumbling from the sky. The next thing William Bruce knew he was falling to earth, along with radio operator T/Sgt Peter Pogovich. They were the only two airmen to survive the ill-fated *Bonnie Vee*.

Fw190 pilot Heinz Papenberg, who had been transferred from the Russian front, was on his first mission since volunteering for the 'Storm group' and closing in on the rear of *Bonnie.* He had armed his 30mm cannon, but as he squeezed the trigger he was greeted by silence. However, remembering the oath they had all sworn to commit to ramming if they had failed to hit the bomber, he decided to put that into effect and got so close to the rear of the bomber he could see the horrified expression on the face of the tail gunner

S/Sgt Glenn Shaffer. Heinz's port wing impacted with *Bonnie*'s tail fin and then he spun out of control. As he jettisoned the heavy cockpit canopy and bailed out, Heinz hit the tail of the Fw190 and badly injured both of his legs, which halted his flying career until nearly the end of the war.

First Lt Ralph Pearson's aircraft, the unnamed, bare, unpainted aluminium 497P-IS, was riddled with holes from cannon shell hits, and the plane's cockpit area took big hits which killed the navigator, 2nd Lt Arthur Stearns, and bombardier Henry Henrikson. The instrument panel in front of co-pilot 2nd Lt Nelson Dimmick disintegrated, fuel poured from the lines into the bomb bay and quickly caught alight. Tail gunner S/Sgt Dwight F. Galyon took a 20mm round to his chest. Luckily his flak vest stopped the exploding fragments and all he received was a severe blow which knocked him backwards. But he recovered and continued to fire at the Fw190s. By this time the aircraft had both No.1 and No.2 engines out and, with the wing blazing furiously, the crippled Liberator slewed away from the rest of the aircraft in the formation. Nelson bailed out and was another to lose his flying boots that day – a violent jolt when he pulled the ripcord saw them disappear into the clouds below. As the bootless Nelson drifted down, a passing German Bf 109 fighter buzzed him and the pilot gave Nelson a cheeky salute. Nelson thought this was not a good way to spend his birthday; his party and his hot date would have to wait.

Flight Engineer T/Sgt Robert Johnson tumbled out of his seat in the top turret where he had been manning the twin 50-calibre guns and fell mortally wounded in a crumpled heap on the floor. Sergeant Harry Tachovsky, the right waist-gunner, who had run out of ammunition and was surrounded by flames, bailed out. For radio operator/gunner T/Sgt O'Keefe the inferno rendered the fire extinguisher useless so, closing his eyes, he had no option but to jump into the burning bomb bay to hit the bomb door opening lever. He felt his skin blister in the heat but, fortunately, the doors opened and he was able to tumble out into the blessed relief of the freezing air at 23,000ft. The 22-year-old from Centralia, Illinois, was certainly having a varied war. He was originally drafted into the infantry where he had become a squad leader in a rifle company and had shone as a baseball pitcher before being accepted into the air force as an air cadet. His dreams of becoming a P51 Mustang pilot were shattered because his blood pressure was slightly over the limit, so he had become a radio operator in the Pearson crew. He was now falling to earth over Siegelshof, but at least he had a better idea of how to survive than a lot of the surrounding aircrew currently hanging from their parachutes, as on his 16th mission he had bailed out over England when receiving the order to do so by miscommunication. He lost his flying boots in the process but had learned from the experience and this time had his GI shoes firmly attached to his parachute harness – along with his K rations – as he fell from the sky. He delayed opening his chute long enough to get out of the ferocious battle going on all around him. He was closely followed by five more of the nine-man crew of the now burning and disintegrating Liberator. After 2nd Lt Ralph H. Pearson had ordered the crew to abandon ship, he tried to keep the aircraft flying as long as possible to give the crew time to get out: 'It was just me and this B-24 cruising along through this beautiful sky. Then, snap! The control wheel went limp in my hands. The elevator cables had burned through. I flung off my oxygen mask and helmet and headed for the bomb bay. As I turned, I suddenly saw Sergeant Johnson behind my seat; he was bent over, buckling on his last leg strap. When he straightened up, I gave him a visual inspection. We only had split seconds as the plane was out of control. I stepped back to my left and waved for him to jump out. He, in turn, waved for me to go.'

Ralph – another of the bootless – landed in a ploughed field to be greeted by angry-looking farmers with pitchforks. But, fortunately for him, some soldiers turned up who were decidedly more humane. They sent the singed Ralph to the local Luftwaffe hospital, leaving the three remaining members of the crew to join the growing death toll.

Following Pearson's aircraft in the lead squadron, both out on the extreme port side, it was 1st Lt Raphael Carrow's *Patches* which was next to go down. With two engines out and a fire in the bomb bay, Raphael decided it was time to go, and rang the alarm bell. The gunners in the back wasted no time getting out from the burning bomb bay. Co-pilot Brainard Newell went out through the nose hatch but, pinned by the G-force in the now spinning aircraft, Raphael struggled to get his harness undone when *Patches* gave up trying to be an airplane, broke in half and left an easy exit for the pilot. Now free from the centrifugal force, and as the burning bomb bay had broken away, all the burnt pilot had to do was step through the hole. Being Jewish, the slightly-singed Raphael, who had lost some of his hair and eyebrows, never carried his dog tags, as the letter 'H' (Hebrew) on them would have ensured a hostile reception from the Nazis. He had lost one of his flying boots when his chute opened, but he was one of those who had tied his shoes to the harness. He landed inside the wire fence of a forced labour camp and was putting his shoes on when the camp guards took him into custody. He was fortunate to be taken to the local Luftwaffe camp, as his co-pilot, who also found himself in a forced labour camp, was to suffer a different fate.

THE BATTLE BEGINS

All the three aborts had come from the 701st Squadron up in the high high right position, so they were already down to seven aircraft before the German attack.

In Liberator 855A, Lt William Dewey, from Detroit, Michigan, was on his eighth mission. He had survived a crash during training when his engine failed in a PT22 basic trainer, but evidence from the engineering officer that it wasn't his fault meant he hadn't been 'washed out' like so many others and had managed to go on to complete his training in Texas. He was awarded his wings in January 1944. Like so many troops heading to the ETO, he was shipped over in a 14-day convoy and had been lucky to get a stateroom for a cabin, unlike the unfortunate enlisted guys jammed into the hold. On arrival in Liverpool he had followed the usual route, shipped to Northern Ireland for additional training about operations in Europe before arriving at Tibenham on 6 August. He had clocked up seven missions in quick succession and expected this to be a 'milk run' when he heard his tail-gunner, S/Sgt Reuben Montanez, say he could see flak and lots of fighters approaching from below and behind. The flak was actually exploding cannon shells from five Fw190s lined up to attack them. Dewey could feel the ship shudder with all the guns firing and the plane took hit after hit. In the attack, Montanez's turret exploded in shards of Plexiglass and a spray of hydraulic fluid. Slightly wounded, he had to get out of what was left of his turret, while both waist-gunners, Bartkow and Johnson, who had been knocked flat by 20mm shells, got up again and returned fire with their .50-cals at the fighters flying alongside. One fighter exploded in a ball of orange flame, but a seven-foot diameter hole appeared in the Lib's fuselage forward of the right waist window, and William Dewey could see a 36" hole in the upper surface of the wing – but the Pratt and Whitney twin Wasp engines were renowned for their ability to take punishment and they kept running. The other William on board, co-pilot 2nd Lt William Boykin, was calling out ships going down one after another when William Dewey asked him to go back to assess the damage as the intercom was out. He returned to report the ship was in bad shape, the gunners were wounded, there were no hydraulics for the controls and the tail looked like it could collapse any moment. Unscathed, nose-gunner S/Sgt Leslie Medlock went back carrying oxygen bottles to help with the wounded, just as a German fighter pilot pulled up close alongside. He flew in the spot where no guns could be brought to bear on him, but dropped away without firing, either out of ammunition or just expecting the ship to go down, and disappeared after a couple of minutes flying in formation with the stricken bomber.

Lt Dewey nursed his aircraft along, but had to slow up to minimize the shaking and started to lose touch with what was now left of the group. He radioed the new leader, Captain Web Uebelhoer, trying to get him to slow up, but to no effect.

On the first pass by the enemy fighters, 2nd Lt Donald Reynolds saw *Little Audrey*'s port inner engine explode in flames. Donald's crew, who had the bad luck to be on their 13th mission, found themselves alone with engines No.2 and No.3 blown to bits. Fortunately they had one working engine each side, which made it easier to control the plane, but the tail turret had taken a direct hit, leaving S/Sgt Harry Twigg with a bloody face from multiple cuts. Waist-gunner Lars Larsen had been mortally wounded and was bleeding badly with radio operator Robert Sheehan trying desperately to staunch the flow. The crippled dull-aluminium Liberator descended slowly through cloud and *Little Audrey* staggered on, heading south-west.

Lt William Dewey at the controls of a Liberator. (Courtesy Linda Dewey)

Out on the port edge of the squadron, 2nd Lt William Golden's *Ole Baldy* was hit by multiple Fw190s, which took out an engine and the tail turret and put a huge hole in the starboard wing. William rang the bail-out bell. In the fuselage, waist gunners Sgts Edward Feltus and Robert Bagley dragged a dazed tail gunner from his shattered turret and pushed the dazed rear gunner out of the back hatch as they received the signal to bail out from the radio operator Sgt Jack Erickson. Erickson was frantically hand-cranking the bomb bay doors but had only managing to get them partially open before top-turret gunner T/Sgt Earl Romine closely followed by co-pilot Lt Christie dived though the narrow opening into the freezing air. Second Lts navigator Edmund Boomhower and bombardier Theo Boecher went out through the nose-wheel doors leaving William Golden at the controls as seven remaining members of the crew managed to jump. It's not known if the tail-gunner Sgt Norman Stewart was unable to operate his parachute because he was incapacitated or it failed, but his body along with the unopened chute was found and buried by a local farmer. He and William Golden paid the ultimate price.

By 10:07 that morning the attacks had largely eased, mainly because the Germans had run short of fuel and ammunition. P51 Mustangs from the 361 Fighter Group had heard the frantic calls for help and arrived to chase off the remaining fighters. A flight of four P38 Lightning fighters also turned up and several dogfights started as they took on the remaining German fighters. S/Sgt Jack Laswell, waist-gunner in Lt Smith's crew, saw four P51s dive into about twenty-five Fw190s who were at a serious disadvantage because of their weight from the armour. They had uprated BMW 801 engines but that meant an accompanying heavy fuel consumption and lack of manoeuvrability. But it was too late to save the group. Lt Leo Lamb, flying a Mustang in the 376 Fighter Squadron, call-sign *Titus Blue 2*, was rammed by an Fw190, was unable to bail out and crashed near Siebleben, adding to the growing list of dead airmen. The toll now stood at more than 100, with more to join them over the next few hours.

In the space of six or eight minutes, the 445th had lost twenty-five Liberators – twenty-three shot down or blown up – leaving wreckage strewn across western Germany near the little villages of Richelsdorf, Willems, Herleshausen and Schiffenberg. Another two American bombers were about to crash-land south of Koblenz, and the remaining B-24s, some badly damaged and with wounded on board, headed west, trying to make for friendly territory.

The German Sturmgruppen retired as well, running low on fuel and ammunition and trying to avoid the pursuing P51 and P38s. They headed back to their bases, having lost 29 fighters with 18 pilots killed and 8 wounded from the return fire of the desperate defending gunners of the 445th and the belated fighter escort.

Heading Home

Of the thirty-eight B-24s which had hauled themselves into the dull, grey sky over Tibenham four hours earlier, 445th now totalled just eleven aircraft still flying. There were four aircraft from the 700 squadron, with Captain Uebelhoer in 547 as the lead crew, the badly-damaged aircraft of Lt Hunter in *Terrible Terry's Terror*, Lt French in *Asbestos Alice* and Lt Heitz in *Bugs Bunny*.

The 701st had just four aircraft left, with Lt William Dewey struggling to keep 855 airborne, Lts Smith and Swofford in 710 E-Easy and *Sweetest Rose of Texas*, and the crippled Liberator *Little Audrey* of Don Reynolds' crew slowly losing height and falling behind.

Hardest hit of all was 702 Squadron. The sole survivor was Lt Stanley Krivic in *Percy*, limping along with three wounded gunners, a feathered propeller, and one engine down on oil pressure and unable to provide much power. Krivic was also unable to maintain altitude and, remembering the morning briefing, was heading for the newly-liberated Brussels airfield. The two remaining 703 Squadron Aircraft of Lt Mercer in 549 and Lt Isom in the relatively unscathed *Patty Girl* brought up the rear.

More than 100 of the Americans who had queued for breakfast in Tibenham that morning were already dead. They had died in a variety of ways: some had gone down with their ships, trapped by centrifugal force and unable to bail out; immolated by burning gasoline; killed by cannon fire; blown out of exploding and disintegrating aircraft and falling to earth either without a chute or with a burning one.

The bomber group had started to split up. Lt Dewey had to decrease his speed to stop his aircraft shaking itself to bits and he could see through the co-pilot's window that with every bump gasoline was sloshing out of the hole in his right wing just behind No.3 engine. Meanwhile Lt Heitz had lost two engines and was slowly descending towards the cloud cover below. But they were all desperate to put Germany as far behind them as quickly as possible.

Having managed to stay airborne for more than one-and-a-half hours by throwing out everything they could, 2nd Lt Donald Reynolds' crew in *Little Audrey* finally ran out of altitude and crash-landed on the side of a hill ten miles south of Koblenz. Despite nearly being decapitated by a torn-off propeller slicing through the fuselage, and trapped by his foot, Robert Sheehan managed to extricate himself with help from engineer Jim Engleman. Then, with the rest of the crew, they managed to release navigator James Withey, who was trapped by his head under the top turret. Gunners Lars Larsen and Bob Long were already dead and, as German soldiers turned up, the surviving seven crew were captured.

Heading just south of west on 250 degrees and then threading their way around the Flak to the south of Koblenz, by 11:20 the Heitz crew had managed to reach the Belgian border and friendly territory. *Bugs Bunny* was starting to lose power in one of her two remaining engines and Lt Heitz saw his only option as a crash landing. He spotted a suitable field about fifteen miles east of Brussels and, knowing they were now in friendly territory, managed to lower the undercarriage and flaps and, using a couple of parachutes as airbrakes, came to a stop with no further damage. Radio operator, Lt Fabian Mack, managed to get the three wounded to a British army hospital with help from some Belgian civilians, but that evening gunner Sgt Louis Ochevsky succumbed to his wounds and joined the ever-growing death toll.

Now down to nine, the rest of the group flew on. First Lt John French, whose aircraft was badly shot up and struggling on two engines, and 1st Lt William Hunter in the badly-damaged *Terrible Terry's Terror*, with a bomb bay awash with leaking fuel, were the next to go down.

The John French crew in *Asbestos Alice* now found themselves alone. The pilots had shut down the Liberator's No.1 engine when it lost a piece of propeller blade. Most of the instruments had ceased to function and the port rudder was shot to pieces and shaking the aircraft so violently they had to shut down No.3 engine as well to reduce the prop-wash over it. As if a gaping hole in the wing near No.2 engine and a bomb bay awash with gasoline weren't enough problems, an Fw190 appeared and lined up for an attack. John thought it was the end of the road when suddenly a P38 appeared and the German dived for the deck with the Lightning in hot pursuit. The American fighter reappeared a few minutes later and tucked in close under the Liberator's wing for a while. With no compasses and damaged maps, navigator Bob Tims used the sun

Lt William Hunter's aircraft, *Terrible Terry's Terror*, which crash-landed in France. (Norfolk Gliding Club archive)

to head generally west to get out of Germany as soon as possible and the P38 gave a waggle of its wings and flew off. Alone again in the slowly-descending aircraft, the crew tried to lighten the ship and slow its descent by dumping any non-essential kit. They started to throw out anything except their parachutes and guns with some of the ammunition, and when this didn't stop the slow loss of altitude, John restarted the feathered No.3 engine and ran it on a low power setting. This slowed the rate of sink and allowed *Alice* to fly out of Germany. When Bob finally managed to identify where they were, they steered a southerly heading towards Reims.

Spotting a P47 Thunderbolt strip, John French lined up on the newly-laid, single-pierced, steel-plank runway which had only come into operation that day. Unable to lower the nose-wheel and with little rudder control, John managed to set the ship down, holding the nose off as long as possible, always worried that sparks would ignite the gas sloshing about in the bomb bay. He was fast running out of elevator authority and could no longer keep the nose off the planks, but fortunately the sparks didn't ignite the fuel fumes and cause an explosion. *Alice* slid to a stop on the side of the strip and the crew evacuated as rapidly as possible, as tail-gunner Herbert Schwartz recounts:

> While the ship was still sliding a little, I jumped 8 feet from the camera hatch and started to run as I was still afraid she would blow up. Greenly and Timms jumped out of the top hatch and ran down top of the ship before props had even stopped. I could have kissed the ground I was so happy and wringing wet with perspiration. A major came over to me and first question asked was "How many injured?" When I told him no one, he stood there in amazement. Everyone complimented French on the landing. It was a remarkable job, but I can honestly say I had full faith in him. About 500 of the field's personnel were out there and they questioned us until a Major picked us up and took us to chow. Before I continue about our experiences on the field, I want to tell the feats of the other men. All the ships accounted for shot down were done by the men in the rear of the ship: Corman, left waist, knocked down 3; Huddleston got one and one "probable." Corman got one ship that came up from the bottom and when he made his breakaway, he got him. I, at this time wanted to be in my original position "the Sperry Ball", but when enemy pilots saw turret was removed, they made attacks at our belly. Another FW had come in about 40 yards off our left wing, and letting his ammo go at lead ship, which our C.O. Major McCoy was flying, he got McCoy as French saw two of his propellers flying thru mid-air, but Corman blasted hell out of this ship and he blew up in mid-air. "Let's hope Major McCoy will rest in peace with a satisfied conscience. He was a real pilot". Corman's 3rd feat was one of the FWs I missed and he got him on the breakaway. Huddleston's feat and "probable" were both breakaways from my tail. Our navigator verified these ships as he said that he lost count of the burning ships he saw go down. He was more scared than any of us and I could hear him tell Greenly over interphone – "steady boy." Our radio man, also unarmed, was going thru fits. Heitz, whom I first believed to be flying off our right wing, was one of the crews that returned safely. I could have sworn he was

shot down, but thank God he wasn't. Three of his men, Palm, Watson, and Chesky, were wounded. This being my original crew, I took particular interest in them. Louis Ochesky was wounded severely receiving wounds in the left shoulder and right leg. Drake tried to quiet him with morphine but he went into hysterics. Palm was hit in the leg – Dr. pronouncing it broken; and Watson who was only man in crew who got credit for a fighter was blown clear out of his turret and wounded in the back. He stamped fire out, however, and might have saved the entire crew. They landed in Brussels. Mack stayed with the wounded in Belgium and rest of the crew returned to the field. (KMHS)

They were all down unharmed – but the 445th was now down to eight flying members.

Next to go down was 1st Lt William Hunter's *Terrible Terry's Terror*. Engineer S/Sgt Bob Ratchford, soaked in gasoline, was working frantically to plug the leaks, knowing that at any moment one spark or tracer round would turn him and the aircraft into an inferno. The old model H B-24, still with the scratched and patched olive-drab paint, had survived many missions but was now running with one engine feathered and was slowly being left by the rest of the group. Fortunately a flight of Mustangs picked the Liberator up and escorted it for a while. When navigator 2nd Lt Robert Keams announced they had crossed into Allied territory the crew breathed a collective sigh of relief. They had flown westwards for more than an hour since the attack and William Hunter knew they were rapidly running out of fuel. They were heading for an airstrip near the town of Willems when another engine suddenly quit and a third starting coughing and spluttering. Hunter picked a field, managed to miss a clump of trees, and clipped some high-tension wires before crash-landing in a potato field. The plane jumped a couple of ditches before the starboard undercarriage dug in and collapsed and *Terrible Terry's Terror* ground-looped and slid to a stop on its belly.

But a bruised and battered crew emerged relatively unscathed.

The Grim Reaper was soon to catch up with most of them. Six months later, while flying on a mission from Hethel to Munster with the 389th Bomber Group, they were hit by a direct flak burst in the wing tanks, and the entire ship immediately erupted in flames. The only survivor from the original crew was tail gunner S/Sgt Fred Schaffe.

But, for now, they were all down safely, and before long French civilians started cautiously approaching the now inert big green monster lying in the middle of the potato field, only to find it was friendly 'Americains' and the crew was soon surrounded by people offering food and drink. In the melee that ensued, one not-quite-so-friendly local managed to 'liberate' a camera from the aircraft, but this was soon discovered and a pursuit retrieved the item from the culprit, who claimed the camera had been given to him as a souvenir. He was soon dragged away by the hostile crowd. The smiles resumed and a flow of Champagne followed for the much-relieved Hunter crew.

That was the last aircraft to go down on the continent while the remaining seven carried on – but not all by choice. The big football-playing pilot 1st Lt Stanley Krivic in *Percy* had intended to land in Brussels, but as they descended through the clouds they were greeted by the sight of the cold, grey North Sea and started throwing out everything they could lay their hands on. Radio operator T/Sgt John Cadden had to restrain them from throwing out the radio on the grounds that he was in touch with air-sea rescue and they could well need their assistance at

Lt William Hunter's *Terrible Terry's Terror* surrounded by French civilians. (Norfolk Gliding Club archive)

any moment. However, with the denser air at low level providing more lift and the now considerably lighter *Percy* descending more slowly, they managed to avoid a watery grave and limped across the Channel heading for home.

Lt Jackson Mercer in the 703rd aircraft 549 and Lt William Dewey in 855 were also crossing the channel. Bill Dewey had decided, with his wounded gunners Bartkow, Johnson and Montanez, it would be better to risk a ditching to get back to England so they could get medical attention quickly. Using the still-working VHF set on the distress channel 'D', he called the codeword 'Colegate' and got a heading from the air-sea rescue service. He was told to check in every fifteen minutes and both badly-damaged aircraft headed for the emergency landing field at Manston on the Kent coast. After an hour they broke through the cloud to the welcome sight of Manston's huge 9000ft and five-times wider than normal runway. By a massive stroke of luck the hydraulics still worked and they managed to lower the flaps and landing gear and, with still-inflated tyres, Bill managed to pull off a 'greaser' landing.

Second Lt William Boykin, co-pilot of 855, was soon to get his own crew, taking navigator 2nd Lt Herbert Bailey with him, but the cruel hand of fate awaited them, as they were both killed when shot down at the end of November, along with four other members of the Wilkins crew, who had escaped death on the disastrous Kassel mission when *Heavenly Body* had aborted and landed on the continent.

Jackson Mercer also managed to get the badly-damaged 549 down intact. With most of the crew completing their thirty missions, they knew they had survived.

Web Uebelhoer in 547 was leading the remaining three aircraft of the 445th: Lt Smith's 710 E-Easy, Paul Swofford in *Sweetest Rose of Texas*, and Lt Isom in an undamaged *Patty Girl*. The decimated group crossed the coast near Ostend at 12:13, heading 295 degrees and starting to let down, crossing the friendly Suffolk coast at Southwold at 3,500ft. When they got back over Tibenham at 12:40, control asked where the rest of the group was, to which Web replied, 'We are the group!' The stunned controller was speechless, but alarm bells rang and crash tenders raced up to the main runway as the battered Liberators made their approaches and landed.

In the control tower commanders General Milton Arnold and Colonel William Jones were astounded at the sight of only four Liberators in the circuit. General Arnold told William the 445th was going to have to stand down next day, to which Colonel Jones replied: 'Hell no, we can't give in. We are going to fly.'

First Lt Paul Swofford in the *Sweetest Rose of Texas* fired a red flare to indicate they had wounded abroad, including himself and the co-pilot Ward Smith. They had both been hit in the face by shards of glass from the shattered windshield. With No.3 engine out and no hydraulics for flaps, the crew hand-cranked the undercarriage down, but with no brakes the *Sweetest* overran the end of the runway and finished up in a ditch.

The others managed to get down safely and taxied back to their hard-standings, where ground crews waited in shock as most of them didn't have aircraft to work on.

The last Liberator still flying was Stanley Krivik's *Percy*. He approached from the south-east with little control and, by the time he had Tibenham in sight, the crippled plane was below 1,000ft and still descending with one engine out and two damaged and not producing much power. With the runways in sight, one of the damaged engines now suddenly quit.

Without hydraulics Krivik was flying by sheer muscle power, using only the cable controls. While the crew tried to crank the main wheels down, engineer Don Bugalecki was in the nose compartment trying to get the wheel down, which he managed after a great struggle. When he got back up

Lt Isom's *Patty Girl*, the only ship fit to fly again the next day. (Norfolk Gliding Club archive)

One of the few to return that day, Paul Swofford's *Sweetest Rose of Texas*. (Norfolk Gliding Club archive)

they all took up their crash positions: the gunners braced against a net in the waist and the radio operator and engineer behind the pilots' seats. Navigator Daniel Dale just sat on the floor in the waist – they all expected to get back down onto Tibenham's welcoming runway shortly.

With no height to do a circuit, Stanley had no choice but to land on the runway in front of him which, instead of the main runway the others had used, was the much shorter runway 33. As the plane got closer to the airfield he saw the runway was covered with maintenance vehicles and, with another disabled aircraft already stopped on it, he had no option but to overshoot. With the extra drag of the undercarriage and no power to climb, all he could do was descend straight ahead and hope the plane would make it to the runway at the next airbase, Old Buckenham, four miles away. But the crippled Liberator didn't quite make it, crashing on a farm half a mile short. *Percy* split in half, the wings were torn off and a blaze started. The impact threw Stanley through the Plexiglass canopy and the big, burly ex-New Jersey football player lay stunned in front of wrecked, blazing *Percy*. Gathering his senses, Stanley got back into the crumpled fuselage and, using all his bull-like strength, pulled co-pilot Leonard Trotta out of the remains of the cockpit – complete with his seat – before returning to the blazing wreck with ammunition starting to 'cook off' and explode all around.

Radio operator John Cadden regained consciousness and, although he was protected by his thick sheepskin flying jacket, he could still feel the heat from the burning wreckage. He looked up from his position, trapped behind the co-pilot's position and pinned under his own radio equipment, and could see the sky. The gunners had been thrown clear when the returning Stanley came and pulled Cadden and engineer Don Bugalecki from the burning wreckage. Krivik's quick-thinking saved their lives and he was awarded the Soldier's Medal for his bravery, but navigator Daniel Dale, who had been catapulted into the wrecked bomb bay, joined the heavy toll of the day's dead.

With that crash, all the aircraft which had departed Tibenham that grey morning were down; 702 squadron had been annihilated and the few remaining aircraft of the three other squadrons were scattered over airfields on the continent and southern England, with just four back where they started.

Krivic crew which crashed at Old Buckenham. (Norfolk Gliding Club archive)

DISPERSAL OF AIRCRAFT DATE 25/9/44 HOURS

DISPERSAL NO.	AIRCRAFT NO.		DISPERSAL NO.	AIRCRAFT NO.	
1	619M		26		
2	166G		27	500R	
2A	497P		28	073Q	
3			29	287I	
4			30	331U	
4A			31	340B	
5			31A	293Z	
5A			32	542A	
6			33	383X	
6A			33A	511Q	319Z
7	784D		34		
8	438L		35	105Q	
9	711B		35A	710E	
10	579N		36	939S	
11	753S		37	922Q	
12	789A		38	294C	
13	549G		38A	609J	
14	342I		39	490Z	
14A	532P		40	863T	855A
15	562U		41	337P	
16			42	940N	
16A	756J		43	707V	
17	541H		44	921B	
18	811E		45	5 79R	
19	2500	355K	46		
20	060U		47		
21	308Q		48	547P	
22	961N	23. 324S	49		
24	985N		50	123A	
25	321Y		51	128R	

HANGAR NO. 1 P47 347P 592N

HANGAR NO. 1 593X P47

RUNWAY 15 022F 810J 078Q 015Q 015I 210U Signed _[signature]_
(FCO on Duty)

From the full aircraft dispersals list of 25 September two days earlier, to the many empty spots on the evening of 27 September 1944.

It was about 1.15 pm. The thirteen wounded were taken from the aircraft and the remaining crew members were surrounded by both the 'brass' and the ground crew, who all asked the same question: 'What the hell happened?'

DISPERSAL OF AIRCRAFT   DATE 27/9/44
1920   HOUR

DISPERSAL NO.	AIRCRAFT NO.			DISPERSAL NO.	AIRCRAFT NO.	
1.	619 M			26	123 P	
2	166 G			27	500 R	
On Grass	P-47 401	P-47 T	C-64	28		
4				29		170
5				30		
6				31 XX	293 Z	985 N
7				32 XX		
8	015 I			33 XX	319 T	
9				34 XX	939 S	
10				35	592 N	
11	753 S			36		
12				37	337 P	921 B
13				38	358 U	
14	593 X			39	294 C	609 D
15				40	480 S	
16	756 J			41		
17				42		
18	811 E			43		
19	250 O			44		
20				45		
21				46		
22				47		
23				48	547 E	
24				49		
25				50	179 N	

HANGAR NO. 1 710 E   562 D   940 W   105 O   347 F   015 Q
HANGAR NO. 2 438 L
RUN. X

Signed _Varyel Backer 2/Lt ac_
(FCO on Duty)
2 Copies - 1 Operations
- 1 Armament

The empty hard-stands bear testimony to the loss the 445th suffered that day. (Norfolk Gliding Club archive)

On the ground in Germany

Just over 100 crew lay dead or dying in Germany, three more lay dead in France, Belgium and Old Buckenham.

One hundred and thirty-two airmen had managed to bail out, some were wounded, some were lying injured, unable to move in fields or swaying gently from parachute shrouds caught in trees. Those who were mobile were trying to bury their chutes and hide, but some were suffering from shock and just sat around waiting to play the hand fate was going to deal them.

Rounding up some of the prisoners, the Germans used a field as an assembly point. Mac Macgregor was deposited there out of the back seat of the little car and, barely able to walk, he limped to join the large group of desolate prisoners. The seriously wounded were sent off for treatment, assisted by a couple of young soldiers. Mac, unable to keep up with the rest of the group, was being walked down the road and, passing a group of Wehrmacht officers, was summoned over to them:

> I was walking down and we came by another little field and there was a guy with a brown uniform and a swastika, a political Nazi guy, and he was over in the field. There were a bunch of Wehrmacht officers there and, all of a sudden, they waved me over. So my guards took me over to the field and the guy in a brown shirt started yelling something at me in German and I have no idea what he was saying. Then he started hitting me under the ear with the back of his hand, he hit me about five or six times and I decided it wouldn't be too smart to hit him back because that would get me in more trouble. I fell against a car, then down on the ground and he starts kicking me in the ribs. I thought that wasn't the right move either. At about that time, the Wehrmacht officers pulled him off, so I got up and I walked a little faster getting away from there,

we were going down the road and, all of a sudden, out of a little cottage over on the right and probably not more than 5' 2", an elderly German with white hair and I think he had a little white beard and he had rubber boots on and he came over and he was spouting something in German and he kicked me in the fanny. That would have been real funny except there was a piece of shrapnel very near where he kicked and aggravated it a little. I still thought it was kind of humorous.

(Courtesy of MacGregor's daughter Mona English)

Trailing the rest of the group, limping along behind, with his two boy soldiers as guards, Mac escaped the clutches of the brown-shirted Nazi and caught up with the rest of the group of prisoners. They were incarcerated in a wire-enclosed chicken coop where they spent the night sleeping on a wooden shelf mostly in a subdued and silent mood as the day's events struck home. The medics turned up and, seeing the shrapnel wounds in Mac's legs, gave him a shot in the shoulder muscle for tetanus. Not being able to communicate that he had already had a shot, he got another, which had some side effects as he recounted:

Anyway, later when I got over to Wetzlar, which is Dulag Luft, my wrists all swelled up and my lips swelled up. It was hives and that's apparently what happened. The medics that were there were British medics and they said, 'Oh, yeah, that's regular'. They gave me a hand full (*sic*) of calcium pills and I took a bunch of them and within six hours it was better.

On his way to the latrine next morning Mac looked up to see the sky full of American aircraft and wondered how the Germans could put up with it.

In the same group was 2nd Lt George Collar from Jackson, Michigan, bombardier of 2nd Lt James Schaen's ship 511 who, at 27, was regarded by his crew as an 'old man'. He had bailed out of his doomed Liberator. As he neared the ground, he saw a man riding a bike towards him. He landed heavily, like Mac, twisting his left ankle, and was dragged backwards across the field by his chute. George finally managed to get the parachute collapsed and, as he lay panting, opened his eyes to find he was staring down the barrel of a Luger pistol.

The limping George was frogmarched off into the village of Lauchröden where, seeing a captured American 'terrorflieger' coming,

81

hostile-looking villagers lined the streets and hurled abuse. One teenager, obviously keen to impress with his bravery, kicked the unfortunate George with his big leather boot. George was marched into the courtyard of the Burgomeister's house and ordered to drop his fur-lined sheepskin flying pants to be searched. As he stood there in his blue, electrically-heated 'Bunnie' long pants with his flying trousers round his ankles, he was attacked by an ugly, irate local farmer with huge fists, who punched him between the eyes and broke his nose. George struggled to get his pants up while fending off further blows and, with his pants secured, he closed with the German to fight back. Then the German grabbed a long-handled spade and swung it at the ducking airman. As the blade whistled over his head, George realized he was fighting for his life and grappled with the farmer for the spade. Just then some of the locals came to George's aid, disarmed the German and, helped by an old man with a huge walrus moustache, the Burgomeister and a local policeman took charge and calmed the mob down. They marched George off to the village church and locked him in the cellar.

The entrance to Lauchröden Church cellar where George and others were imprisoned. (Author's collection)

First Lt Ira Weinstein, known to his squadron as Jerry, wasn't having a good day either. The previous day he had led a disorderly group on a weapons carrier into Norwich, where they had attended a 6 pm service at the Corn Hall for the Jewish Day of Atonement. There he had atoned for seventy-seven sins, giving him carte-blanche to be bad for the next year – a state of affairs which had now come home to roost. Considering it was the Yom Kippur holiday, he could have had the day off; he already had a three-day pass and could have been in London having a good time. Instead he was dangling from a parachute over Nazi Germany.

At only 5ft tall, the little guy from Chicago needed only one more mission to finish his tour. As an early member of the Tibenham group, he had missed the new requirement to do 30 missions and only had to do 25. He wanted to get back to America in time for his wife's birthday at Christmas. As a lead crew navigator and bombardier, he was required to attend every briefing and, thinking today's mission wasn't going to be too bad with the fighter cover, he had gone to commanding officer Colonel Jones and begged to be put on the list to fly. Col Jones told him he was being stupid but, after much pleading, agreed in the end to let him go. So, no longer having an assigned crew, he had joined the ill-fated 702 Squadron's 1st Lt Myron Donald's crew in *Flossye*. He acted as bombardier that day and was manning the front turret when navigator Eric Smith pulled him backwards from it. Ira saw him bail out through the nose-wheel doors of the burning aircraft but, as he tried to follow Eric out he got hung up with his backpack chute strap. Ira had to haul himself back into the aircraft to free himself from the strap, which was caught on the bombsight. Having freed himself he managed to jump clear of the now spinning *Flossye* to pull his ripcord about 2,500ft above the ground. His flying boots flew off and disappeared and Ira, along with George Collar, now wished he had wired his shoes to the parachute harness.

Ira landed in some hills, dumped his chute and ran to hide in a nearby pinewood. But he was soon picked up and taken into custody, placed in a cell with about twenty other prisoners, and there was reunited with George Collar.

The Germans soon started to make use of the prisoners. Carl Sollien had to use his pianist's hands to pull the headless corpses of his gunners and flight engineer from the rear of the wreck of his *Fort Worth Maid*. Second Lt John Dent's body was still in the nose turret and co-pilot 2nd Lt William Koenig lay dead not far away. The Germans sent out a detail with two horse-drawn hay wagons escorted by a mixture of about ten old men and Hitler youth armed with a motley collection of weapons including shotguns and arms dating from the First World War. This strange party was sent out with the wagons to collect corpses and guns from the wreckage which now lay scattered over a wide area of this mainly-agricultural part of Germany. Led by an aristocratic old German mounted on a horse and carrying a shotgun acting as a scout, the men, including George Collar, engineer T/Sgt George Eppley from the Schaen crew, and an unidentified member from another group, marched down the street and out into the countryside to begin their grim task.

The first body to be found, face down in a little orchard, was that of 2nd Lt Herbert Bateman, navigator for the Johnson crew in the 703 Squadron aircraft *Fridget Bridget*. When a 20mm cannon shell hit the Liberator, Bateman had fallen out of the blown-off nose wheel doors and, despite the best efforts of bombardier 1st Lt James Dowling to hang onto his legs, he had fallen to earth without his parachute. The corpse – with every bone broken – was still warm when it was found and loaded onto the cart. In the middle of an open field, surrounded by a pool of blood from his nearly severed leg, they found S/Sgt Joseph Gilfoil. He had been dropped from Reg Miner's aircraft on a static line to open his chute, in the vain hope of saving his life. While the parachute had deployed and he was alive when he hit the ground, nobody had found Joe before he bled to death and his pale-blue-and-white bloodless body joined Bateman's in the haywain.

Coming across the wreckage of *Big Jane*, the B-24 of the Walther crew, they found the bottom half of co-pilot 2nd Lt Martin Geiszler still strapped in his seat. The top half of the big man from Bell, California, was 100 yards away, wedged in a tree. The body of radio operator T/Sgt Glenn Bergquist lay nearby. The only survivor of *Jane* was the pilot, 1st Lt Edgar Walther. The aircraft had blown up in mid-air and he woke up in a German hospital with no idea how he got there. The bodies of the rest of the crew joined the ever-increasing pile in the back of the wagons. They found more bodies and body parts and, as the search continued at another crash site, they extricated a gunner from his turret with the top of his head missing. Another lay dead in his chute with his feet in a stream. The grim task continued until the evening when, with more than a dozen corpses and body parts in the two hay wagons, they got to the cemetery at Lauchröden. There they unhitched the horses, left the two wagons standing next to a stone building, marched into town and went straight up to the village pump where they assuaged their raging thirst. They hadn't had a drink of water all day and the only food they had to eat was a couple of apples a small child had given them.

The prisoners were marched back to the little jailhouse again and, in the gathering dusk, they were given some white bread and a big mug of ersatz coffee. It was the last white bread George Collar saw until he got back to the

United States ten months later. Rousted out in the middle of the night, their tasks started again when a grey Wehrmacht truck pulled up outside with wounded men on board. George and the others climbed in and set off on a tour around the local area collecting more wounded from the barns, mills and buildings where they lay and took them to the hospital at Eisenach. The three unwounded were taken to a guard room on an army base, where they were reunited with about twenty-five captured members of the 445th, including Ira Weinstein and Mac MacGregor, both of whom lamented that their final missions hadn't gone as planned.

Second Lt William Bruce had delayed his drop from the disintegrating *Bonnie Vee* to avoid being shot at. But he was so low when he pulled his ripcord he could see a farmer ploughing his field. He wound up with his right leg hung over a branch in a tall tree, with burning plane wreckage falling all round him and setting some of the wood on fire. With great difficulty William managed to untangle himself and get down from the tree but, unable to stand, in pain and covered in blood, he crawled for hours until he eventually found a farmhouse and managed to attract the attention of the occupants, a man and two women. They washed the blood from his face and tried to give him some aid, carried him inside and gave him a very welcome drink of milk. Then a young boy came in and pointed a rifle at William. The man knocked the gun from the boy's hands and he sped off, only to return with seven armed soldiers who threatened William until it was discovered he wasn't armed and was, indeed, unable to stand.

When they discovered they weren't getting very far with their interrogation, the soldiers put William in a horse-drawn farm cart and paraded him through the village, where the road was lined with a hostile, spitting, stone-throwing crowd. He was put in a small barn, with the crowd still baying outside, and left there for several hours. The soldiers returned and resumed the interrogation, breaking William's jaw in the process. Eventually he was carried by four soldiers to a train for a three-day journey to the PoW detention centre at Frankfurt. By this time William was bruised from head to toe and almost paralysed.

Generally it was better to fall into the hands of the military rather than civilians. Some crew members of 2nd Lt Howard Jones's *Roughhouse Kate* had a hostile reception from locals. Gunner Willis Meier from St. Louis, Missouri, had to draw his Colt 45 pistol to avoid getting his throat cut before handing the gun over to a Luftwaffe soldier and surrendering. Locals were beating Milton Lee, the wounded nose-turret gunner, to death when a soldier rescued him by firing his automatic rifle to warn off the mob baying for blood.

The Inquest

Back at Tibenham that afternoon, the inquest had started. Jimmy Stewart, the ex-commander of the 703rd Squadron, hearing of the disaster had come over from group headquarters at Kettering Hall about seven miles away, and was visibly upset as he listened to Web Uebelhoer's account of the disastrous raid.

The tall, lean, 36-year-old movie star, James Maitland Stewart, newly-promoted to captain, had learned to fly, as a private pilot, in 1938 and had joined the USAAF in March 1941. He had served for two years as a multi-engine instructor and it was then he met and became good friends with the now Major Donald McCoy, who had followed a similar path in getting a flying licence at the age of 16. Jimmy Stewart had always wanted to get into combat, and had used his status to 'pull some strings' with Col 'Pop' Arnold, commander of the training base at Boise, Idaho. Pop Arnold was friends with Colonel Terrill, who was forming a new heavy-bombardment squadron, designated the 445th, at the Idaho base. Jimmy was accepted as commander of the 703rd Squadron and busied himself with the logistics of getting the group over to Europe by the southern route – via the Caribbean, South America and North Africa. He finally touched down in Lt John Sharrard's Liberator *Tenovus,* the sixth Liberator of the 445th group to land at Tibenham, on 24 November 1943.

It was on that trans-Atlantic mission that Lt Poor's B-24 *Sunflower Sue* was lost with all its crew and passengers somewhere over the Caribbean. That loss was a big blow for the newly-formed 703rd.

James Stewart led twelve combat missions before he was promoted and sent six miles away to the 453rd at Old Buckenham, where he was group operations officer. But he was only there from March to July before he was promoted again to Lieutenant Colonel and made chief of staff to the 2nd Combat Wing at their HQ in Ketteringham Hall. The huge manor house, set in acres of grounds, was still only seven miles from Tibenham and Jimmy

Jimmy Stewart walking from the mess hall. (Norfolk Gliding Club archive)

maintained close ties with the Group at Tibenham airfield and surrounding villages. He paid frequent visits both to the Officers Club – and a local lady friend – and was frequently seen banging out the song *Ragtime Joe* on the club's battered piano, surrounded by adoring ladies and high-ranking officers keen to bathe in his limelight. He didn't know, however, that he was sharing a girlfriend with Isom's navigator, 1st Lt Art Shay!

The other pianist in the club, Carl Sollien, and his best friend and bombardier Malcolm MacGregor – Mac to his friends – would quite often meet with Jimmy, as Mac relates:

> That's how I got to know Jimmy Stewart – Carl's playing. Jimmy sat down next to me one day and asked if I wanted some bourbon, which was tough for us to get. We got to talking and he asked how many missions I'd flow. I said I had five, and then I asked him, 'And how many have you flown, Sir?' He had flown 13.
>
> (Norfolk Gliding Club archive)

Jimmy Stewart playing in the Officers' Club. (Norfolk Gliding Club archive)

Red Cross workers set up a portable phonograph to entertain the men of the 445th BG at their base at Tibenham. (NARA)

But there was no laughter on the day the remnants of the Kassel raid returned, as Jimmy and the rest of the commanders stood in silence on the cool, grey concrete of hard-stand 48 listening to the accounts of the catastrophe that had befallen the 445th and his beloved 703 Squadron. Among the missing was his good friend Don McCoy, although Jimmy was probably hoping Don had either crash-landed in France and would turn up somewhere or was at least a PoW. He didn't know that both Don and Captain John Chilton lay dead in Germany, still strapped into their seats in the wrecked cockpit of 541, along with the nearby bodies of navigator 1st Lt Raymond Ische and co-pilot 2nd Lt Harold Sutherland.

The surviving crews at Tibenham helped unload the wounded into ambulances, which left for the base sick quarters and took the more seriously wounded to the hospital at Quidenham. Then everybody went to the operations room for a coffee and a more formal debrief and to fill in combat reports and surrender navigators' logs for the inevitable inquiry.

Jimmy Stewart on the Tibenham control tower. (Norfolk gliding Club archive)

It was the 'second time around' for the staff officers of the 445th.. The previous February, on a deep penetration mission to bomb the Messerschmitt factory at Gotha and with no long-range fighter escorts available at that time, German fighters had decimated the group. Thirteen of the twenty-nine aircraft dispatched were shot down and lost – nearly 45 per cent, a horrendous result. But the Kassel mission had a loss rate of 77 per cent, which was almost beyond belief.

Navigator Lt Frank Federici's crew had just returned from ferrying a colonel to Scotland. As they landed they saw all the empty spaces on the hard-stands and were puzzled as to where all the aircraft had gone. Frank walked over to the crew chief and asked, 'Where are all our ships?' He replied, 'We've been wiped out, Sir.' Frank, somewhat irritated, retorted, 'That's not funny, Sergeant,' to which the sergeant replied, 'Honest to God, Sir' – and burst into tears! Feeling bad, Frank took several minutes to comfort the very distressed man.

The inquest continues. S/Sgt Thomas Spera, a photo observer, (standing 2nd from the left) was lucky to return from the crash landing in France on Lt Hunter's *Terrible Terry's Terror.* (NARA)

Crews grab a welcome cup of coffee before heading to the debriefing. Art Shay (raising a cup to his lips, centre) pictured after an earlier mission. (© Art Shay Archive)

Back in Germany it was early afternoon and the killing hadn't ended. More than 130 American airmen had managed to bail out successfully, and while some, particularly the wounded, were unable to escape and were captured straight away, others tried to avoid the irate German civilians and went into hiding, mainly in the plentiful areas of woodland. Many had taken to their heels, trying to cover the 250 miles separating them from the Allied front lines and safety. Some managed to evade capture for nearly a month, but none made it back successfully.

Three members of 1st Lt James Baynham's crew in 702 squadron's *King Kong* – 2nd Lts navigator John Cowgill, bombardier Hector Scala and radio operator T/Sgt James Fields – had come down near the town of Nentershausen. James had only just landed by parachute when he was shot and killed by a soldier, called Rubsman, who happened to be home on leave.

Second Lt Newell Brainard, co-pilot of 1st Lt Carrow's aircraft *Patches*, suffered a head injury when he landed nearby and was taken to

THE KASSEL RAID, 27 SEPTEMBER 1944

Baynham crew. (Norfolk Gliding Club archive)

a local house where a Red Cross nurse bandaged his head. T/Sgt John Donahue, radio operator of *Clay Pidgeon*, had also come down in the area and the pair were kept in an apartment building in Nentershausen until they were collected by Gestapo agents Hellwig and Eggert. They were then taken to 'Ostarbeitslager', a forced labour camp for Russian prisoners who were mining copper. In the headquarters conference room, the Gestapo men were joined by a willing group of volunteers to form an impromptu execution squad. The squad included camp commander Josef Ehlen, foreman Franz Mueller, miner August Viehl, local policeman Martin Baesse, Reinhard Beck, a local baker, and mining inspector Paul Winkler. After being repeatedly interrogated and beaten with fists, a chair leg and a bottle, the two airmen were taken outside and shot in the back of the head with pistols. A call from the nearby village of Suess that two more airman were being held in the local church saw the Gestapo men and the miner drive there quickly. They administered beatings to John Cowgill and Hector Scala, both from 1st Lt James Baynham's *King Kong*, before taking them back to the conference room at the camp, where the same treatment was meted out to them. They too were taken out and shot.

Their bodies, along with those of Brainard and Donahue, were then dumped in a communal grave in the local cemetery.

Hanging from a tree by his parachute, Eugene George, his face swollen with blisters from burns sustained in the burning bomb bay of *Eileen* when his partly-melted oxygen mask had stuck to his face, could hear explosions as the ammunition in a nearby crashed aircraft started cooking off in the flames. Swinging in his harness until he reached the tree trunk, Eugene was able to climb up to free the entangled parachute. Looking down he could see two foxes, with red coats and white tips to their tails, set off into dense undergrowth. George climbed down and set off along the same trail as the foxes. He managed to hide and take out his escape kit, only to find the map was missing.

Also hanging from a tree in the same wood was 2nd Lt Corman Bean, navigator in the Schaen crew. From Fargo, North Dakota, Bean was on his 16th mission and had bailed out from the 702 squadron Liberator 511, which was blazing from wings to tail. Only crewmen in the front of the fuselage had survived, the waist and tail gunners were incinerated in the inferno. Free-falling on his back until he passed through the clouds, he had witnessed the battle happening above him before pulling the ripcord on his chest parachute, and he now found himself swinging gently and unhurt about forty feet above the ground. Pulling himself up so he could release the straps, and then climbing down, he was greeted by Eugene George. As a navigator Corman at least had an idea where they were and had a map and small compass, so together they set off, heading west for the Allied lines. Travelling mainly at night and following an *Autobahn*, they carried on for two nights, avoiding German troops searching in vehicles and on bicycles, before realizing the hopelessness of the situation and surrendering to a farmer who took them to the local Luftwaffe base where they joined the swelling numbers of captured airmen. Eugene wound up being transported by rail to Frankfurt City Hospital where his burns were treated.

All the crew of 2nd Lt Palmer Bruland's *Texas Rose* had managed to bail out of the 701 Squadron aircraft safely, the wreckage falling near Schiffenburg, and Palmer, along with navigator 2nd Lt Norman Cuddy and gunner S/Sgt Charles Dove, managed to evade immediate capture, while co-pilot 2nd Lt Peter Belitsos, radio operator T/Sgt James Boman, flight engineer S/Sgt Steven Gray, and gunner Sgt Hugh Sullivan were all picked up straight away and were now 'in the bag'. T/Sgts Ferdinand Flach and Lee Huffman, both gunners, came down together in woodland near the village of Hattenrod. There they were discovered by a young woman called Anna Kutscher, out walking with her infant son. She took them to the local Burgomeister. From his office they were collected, separately, by Lt Herman Noack, a disabled member of the airborne infantry, and Karl Boess, a butcher by trade and part-time member of the local fire brigade.

The first airman was put in Boess's car and driven off, ostensibly to the local airbase at Giessen. En-route the car turned into a sideroad and the flier was ordered out and told to walk ahead of Noack. He was shot in the back three times and, after taking his shoes and leaving the body, the Germans set off back to the Burgomaster's office to collect the other airman, who was still under guard. They followed the same routine as before and the airman was told to show them where his parachute was. He was driven towards the forest at Lich, ordered out of the car and, walking towards the wood, he was also shot in the back. The pair then returned to Hattenrod, collected two men and shovels and went to bury the first corpse. They then repeated the process for the second corpse, but with two different men, telling all involved that the fliers had been shot while trying to escape and to keep their mouths shut about the affair.

Second Lt Harold Allen, co-pilot in 2nd Lt Howard Jones's ship *Roughhouse Kate*, came down by parachute near Döringsdorf. After being brutally beaten up by a civilian, he was taken to Eschwege airfield hospital where he died of internal injuries at 18:15. With the other murdered airmen at Nentershausen, these killings brought the total death toll to 115, and still rising.

Navigator 2nd Lt William Flickner was on the run with 1st Lt Richard Fromm, the pilot of Liberator 080. They had met on the ground. William had bailed out of *Fridget Bridget* and joined the ranks of airmen on the run from the now alert Germans, who had mobilized several search teams from local troops and the *Volkssturm*, the German equivalent of the Home Guard. They were joined by a group of Hitler youth tasked to collect Allied propaganda leaflets which had been widely scattered round the region.

The airmen had never been given parachute training – just a briefing on how to free-fall out of trouble and when to pull the ripcord. This was why many of those who had bailed out had broken bones and sprained ankles on landing. By now many crewmen had been picked up and were incarcerated in local jails, churches and Burgomeisters' offices and, as the day wore on, they were being brought together into groups. The rest were still trying to evade capture.

Because of his previous bail-out experience, a youth spent hunting in the woods, and recent army training, one of the better-equipped to survive a bailout and escape undetected was Pearson crew radio operator Doyle O'Keefe. Once out of his crippled plane, Doyle had spread his arms and legs to stop his body tumbling and stabilise his descent. He had lost a flying boot, cap and goggles and was free-falling on his back, delaying his chute opening, when he witnessed the doomed and blazing aircraft from which he had so narrowly escaped break apart. The starboard wing collapsed in the Liberator's death throes, adding to the picture of blazing wreckage and parachutes descending over the picturesque German countryside. Doyle was in free-fall for nearly two minutes until the clouds blotted out the fantastic spectacle. Then with a jerk he pulled his ripcord and descended, unseen, to the ground.

He quickly gathered the chute and headed for the trees, where he buried it after detaching his shoes from the harness. He decided to lay low and quickly climbed a lookout tower to ensure he hadn't been seen and no pursuers were in sight, before he hid in some brushwood until dark. With his shoes, escape kit and a packet of 'K' rations for sustenance, he was certainly in better shape than the rest of the crewmen now scattered over the countryside. Apart from a blistered face from the burns he suffered before he got out of the Liberator, he was at least able to move quickly and quietly across country. He headed west.

The wood where T/Sgt Doyle O'Keefe hid before boarding the freight train. (Author's collection)

THE KASSEL RAID, 27 SEPTEMBER 1944

The problem with moving westwards was that lots of streams and rivers in that part of the Germany ran on a north-south axis and bridges were guarded, so Doyle kept moving through the night. After a close encounter with a night watchman and a day lying low on the edge of a freight yard, he managed to get aboard a freight train heading west for several hours over all the bridges and autobahns. His train was held up for an armaments train carrying tanks and half-tracks and, swapping trains, Doyle managed to secrete himself in a half-track. Using a match to light his way he sat at the map-reading table in the cabin, where it was warm and dark, and he soon fell asleep. He woke up to find he was in a freight yard close to a town, decamped and, evading the guards, set off west again – but not before leaving an empty English book of matches for the new occupants of the half-track to find. It amused him to wonder what the German soldiers would think when they took delivery.

He hid for another day, then set out again on foot, only to come upon a group of ladies who, suspicious of his burned face, alerted a soldier and his guard dog and the unfortunate Doyle was taken into custody. Another one 'in the bag'.

Twelve-year-old schoolboy Walter Hassenpflug was with his class-mates outside his school, which had recessed as air-raid sirens sounded, when they heard the sound of aircraft and cannon fire from above. They couldn't see anything through the overcast sky until the debris of an exploding Liberator fell to earth, with the distinctive twin-rudder assembly making it easily identifiable to the knowledgeable Walter. He also spotted several parachutes floating down to earth. It was potato harvesting time, so the fields had lots of workers in them gathering in the crop and most of the landing aircrew were soon captured and the wounded taken to the hospital at Bad Hersfeld.

One of the chutes had Reg Miner hanging in its straps. Reg landed close to his burning ship. The 1st Lt from New Jersey had survived his 20th and last mission, but he was arrested immediately on landing and taken, bruised and shoeless but OK, to the local police chief's house, where he was kept for several hours while the chief made telephone inquiries about what to do with him. While this was going on, several locals came to see the captured flier and, since some of them had been to America, they were keen to chat to him. One of the locals was carrying Reg's missing flying boots, which had been recovered from close to the wreckage. Later Reg was taken to the railway station where he met more locals – but this time they were hostile. One slapped him on the forehead before being restrained by the police chief, who pushed Reg onto a train bound for the next town, where the chief walked him to the local jail and he was put in a cell on his own. The rest of Reg Miner's crew had managed to bail out successfully, but Joe Gilfoil was bleeding to death in a field and co-pilot 1st Lt Virgil Chima had come down in the middle of a big beech wood where his corpse, curled up in the foetal position, wasn't discovered until two months later. His parachute had been cut off and the cause of his death was unknown.

The remaining ten crew members had landed successfully but several were wounded. Tail gunner Alvis Kitchens had broken his ankle as well as being wounded in the backside. Gunner S/Sgt Larry Blowers also had back wounds and bombardier 1st Lt John Omick had a broken leg, but at least they were down alive. They were soon captured. Radio operator 2nd Lt Henard Branch, navigator 2nd Lt Charles Jackson and engineer T/Sgt Robert Ault had all landed unhurt and joined the ranks of those trying to evade capture as they took off into the woodland.

First Lt Frank Bertram, the navigator, counted himself lucky. He had a brand-new parachute and harness which had worked faultlessly and, armed with his prayer book and lucky charm baseball mitt stuffed into the pockets of his new gabardine flying suit, he had come down in a wood, snapping branches as he fell through the trees before hitting the ground with enough force to knock himself out. When he came to, surrounded by his chute at the bottom of a tall pine tree, it was a few minutes before the feeling came back into his feet and legs and he could hobble away wearing just his felt electric flying boots as, like many others, he didn't have any shoes wired to his harness. Frank was in pain, with his back, knees and feet hurting, but he managed to gather up his parachute and hide it under branches, and set off stumbling along down a forest road. He had to duck off the road to avoid being spotted by soldiers out looking for the downed Americans. They were travelling in a coughing, spluttering truck which spewed clouds of black smoke because it was powered by the gas generated by burning coal. When they had passed, Frank carried on working his way through the woods, avoiding a farmer ploughing his fields with a pair of heavy horses. He crossed an autobahn and, regaining the woods the other side, came upon a hide used by hunters. As it was now getting dark, he settled down for the night, trying unsuccessfully to keep warm using branches as a covering.

S/Sgt Wilbur Brown was unconscious and had no idea how he had bailed out from the burning *Our Gal*. He revived briefly and, badly burned, managed to deploy his parachute, only to find it was attached by just one strap. He then lapsed back into unconsciousness and landed in a field where he was greeted by hostile farm workers armed with pitchforks. A German soldier on a motorcycle then took him to the local hospital. There his badly-burned face was treated, but the injuries had left him nearly blind. It was going to be a long time and several operations and skin grafts before his sight was fully restored.

Back at Base

Back at Tibenham, the unwounded members of the four surviving crews of Uebelhoer, Smith, Swofford and Isom, had all been locked away and debriefed by Jimmy Stewart. He had listened intently to the reports and experiences with tears in his eyes and had needed a few moments away from the crews to compose himself. The navigators' logs had been confiscated and it had taken hours to fill in all the combat reports before, finally, the crews were released to get some dinner.

In the dining hall that evening a couple of dozen crew members sat in a room set for more than 200. The meal was a quiet, solemn occasion.

The empty tables and benches bore grim testimony to the day's calamity and those who had sat there for breakfast and now lay dead, captured or on the run in Germany. After a sombre and very quiet meal, the surviving crews returned to their huts, some of which had only one crewmember in, or, like the Miner/Schaen hut, now stood completely empty.

Never again would Reg Miner's co-pilot Virgil Chima make a date with the little blonde telephonist from the Norwich telephone exchange; he now lay dead in a wood in Germany with his laughing, black eyes glazing over. Pilot Carl Sollien's fingers wouldn't be playing *Begin the Beguine* on the officers' mess piano as he was now heading for a prison camp along with little Jerry Weinstein, who wouldn't be yelling for a beer at the bar he could hardly see over. In the space of one day the world at Tibenham had changed, but there was no room for sentiment and tears. The war wasn't going to wait and the 445th would have to get on with the job.

Out on the airfield twenty-nine hard-stands also stood empty with redundant ground crews milling around trying to assist those crews who now had badly-damaged aircraft to repair. 710 E-Easy, *Betty, FiFi/Nella, Sweetest Rose of Texas* and *Rambling Wreck* were all so badly damaged on this and previous missions that they had been put into the two large, green T2 Hangars for major repairs rather than it being done out on the hard-stands. In total,

BACK AT BASE

THIS PAGE IS UNCLASSIFIED

COMBAT FORM

Group **445**

Squadron **703**

A/C No. **811**

Date **SEPT 27, 1944**

Place where attacked **8 MI N. OF EISENACH**

Time **1001** height **21,000**

1. Story of the attack: FW-190 CAME FROM BEHIND, UNDERNEATH; WHEN HE WAS PULLING OUT IN FRONT OF NOSE AT 50 YARDS, NOSE TURRET FIRED, FOLLOWED E/A AROUND TO RIGHT. E/A EMITTED BLACK SMOKE, E/A PILOT BAILED OUT AT ABOUT 150 YARDS.

(Include above how a/c attacked; how close he came; where he was hit; how much he was damaged; and how he looked and acted going away. Also color, markings or information of interest or interest concerning e/a.)

2. Diagram of attack:

On diagram, show:
a. Which of our a/c was attacked; e.g. (X)
b. Direction of e/a attack; e.g. →
c. Sun position; e.g. ☼

Data on Combat
a. Our heading **240**
b. Visibility **EXCELLENT**
c. Type of e/a **FW-190**
d. Level of attack:
above
level **X**
low

3. Credit Desired For: Position **NOSE TURRET**
Full
Rank **2ND LT.** Name **SHAY, ARTHUR** A.S.N. **0887102**

Home address: **1402 BRONX RIVER AVE** City **BRONX, N.Y.**

4. Witnessed by Pilot--Co-Pilot--Nav--Bomb--L.W.--R.W. Top T.--Ball T.--Tail G.

5. Also hit by Pilot--Co-Pilot--Nav--Bomb--L.W.--R.W.--Top T.--Ball T.--Tail G.

6. Comments by Interrogating Officer:
PILOT, BOMBARDIER AND BOTH WAIST GUNNERS SAW THE E/A PILOT BAIL OUT

Credit Suggested:
N.C.
Damaged
Probable
Destroyed **XX**

Signature of Interrogating Officer
F. A. JACOBI, 1ST LT. AC

Additional Remarks: DEST

Art Shay's combat report.

99

twenty-nine bombers still remained at Tibenham, but fewer than half were serviceable. Of the aircraft to return to Tibenham that day, only Lt Isom's *Patty Girl* remained serviceable enough to fly again the next day.

In his hut, Art Shay wrote a quick note to his girlfriend, Florence, getting the facts a little wrong, as in fact four aircraft had returned to base. They married just over a month later.

Darkness was starting to fall when Bill Dewey's crew, in a B-24, which had been repaired at Manston and borrowed from the 491st bomber group at North Pickenham, returned to the now fairly deserted black asphalt at Tibenham. After debrief and getting some chow, Bill headed for his hut

One of the mess halls at Tibenham. Local ladies were employed as waitresses and cooks. (© Art Shay Archive)

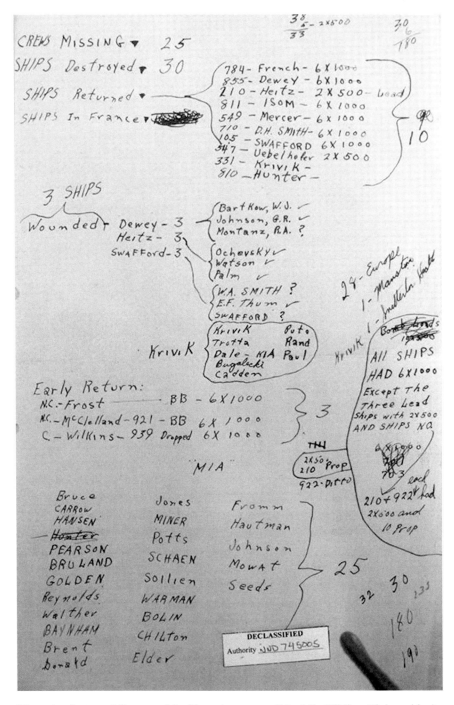

The grim facts and figures of the Kassel carnage. (Norfolk Gliding Club archive)

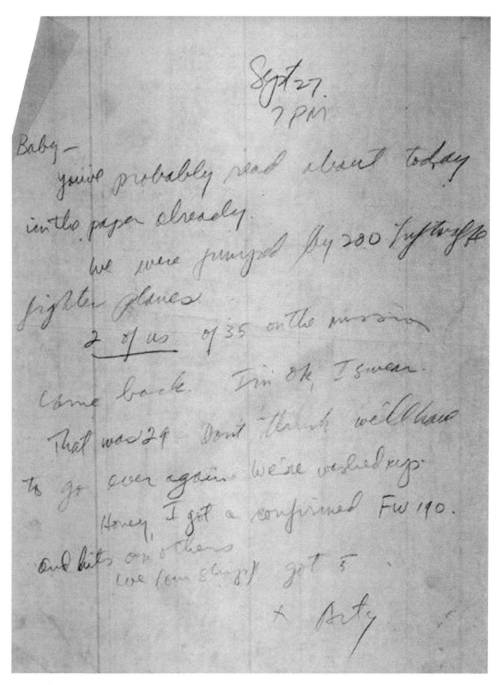

Art Shay needed few words to tell his girlfriend of the fateful raid. (© Art Shay Archive)

The NCOs' club bar at Tibenham airfield. (Norfolk Gliding Club archive)

where he met a despondent Lt Keith Frost who had aborted in *Slossie* with a sick crew member that morning. Keith intended to 'pack it in' having been unnerved by a bad crash-landing at Manston in October. However, he was dissuaded from throwing in the towel and flew another nine missions before crashing again, near Tibenham, on 10 November when he got back from a mission to Hannau. He went on to fly two more missions, taking his total to sixteen before finishing.

Near Reims, in France, an amazed and unharmed crew walked round the now quietly ticking *Asbestos Alice* as the remaining gas drained away. As it became safer to venture closer, they inspected their broken bird, riddled all over with holes from 30 and 50-calibre ammunition. There were larger holes caused by exploding cannon shells and, with the busted fuel and hydraulic lines and crumpled nose, *Alice* was a sorry sight. After marvelling at their narrow escape they grew tired and were then transported to a large local chateau, which was the officers' quarters of the P47 fighter group they had dropped in on. They headed straight for the bar and had several large whiskies as they discussed what had happened to their compatriots and wondered who had managed to bail out.

It wasn't only the Americans who were shocked and devastated by the events of that fateful Wednesday. In the eleven months since their arrival, the nearly 3,000 'Yanks' had had a massive impact on the local population of the villages of Tibenham, Tivetshall, Aslacton and Great Moulton. Largely untouched by the dangers of war, apart from the occasional V1 buzz bomb flying overhead and a strafing attack by the odd German aircraft, the only time bombs fell in the vicinity of the airfield, it was the Americans, not the Germans to blame. Early in the afternoon of 22 February 1944, aircraft of the 92nd bombardment group heading back to their base at Podington were passing over Tibenham. Suddenly there was a terrific explosion. A couple of bombs had accidentally been released from one of the planes and they fell just outside living site number 3 in Aslacton, occupied by men of the 462nd Base sub-depot. Two enlisted men were killed, S/Sgt Lester McCormick and Sgt William Daly, several were wounded, and damage was done to the buildings in the site. In addition Mrs Cook, the wife of a nearby farmer, was killed as she sat opposite her husband in the kitchen of their farmhouse at Hill farm. She fell over dead practically into the arms of her husband. It was a tragic accident.

They were all rural communities, many of the houses having no running water and lit by gas lamps, and most local employment was either agricultural or at the Maltings at Tivetshall. The work was poorly paid in comparison to the average American airman, with a local farm labourer earning two or three pounds a week, compared to a S/Sgt on nearly £11 – officers earned considerably more. So it wasn't long before the locals started to benefit from, and in some cases exploit, the American servicemen. Local farms provided some extras to the diet; eggs would sometimes change hands at exorbitant prices to a GI unfamiliar with English pounds, shillings and pence. Local ladies might receive an English pound and a bar of precious soap to do a complete load of airman's washing, or seven shillings and sixpence for just a pair of overalls that way they could earn the equivalent of a week's rent on a local council house, but it was hard work because the water had to be carried from the well and boiled in a copper vessel over an open fire.

This extract from the diary of Lt Robert J. Toeppe shows he thought he had a good deal trading with the locals:

> Slept late and had a nice roast pork dinner today. We took some pictures and Hasselbach and I went bicycle riding around the countryside and took more pictures. Found a place to buy some

eggs and a chicken. Got a dozen eggs for only 5 Shillings and a chicken for 26 Shillings. Our laundry lady is going to roast it for us the first of the week. I'll bet it will be good. Had a few more letters today, from the Elks Club. The fellows flew to Bonnieres again today. Everyone got back OK, but the bombing was poor.

The base also brought direct employment to the local civilians. Construction and maintenance was always going on and the canteens employed local ladies to assist, with many working twelve-hour shifts. Local pubs, like The Railway and The Greyhound, became watering holes for Americans as well as the locals and many a game of darts was played between the locals and the Yanks with a pint of warm British beer at stake for the winner.

Mr Carver, a local farmer, used a horse and cart to provide a local taxi service, meeting nearly every train at Tivetshall railway station and ferrying the amused Americans back though the checkpoints. He was so well known he only had to call out his pass number to get onto the base without stopping.

Woodrow Lane, Aslacton, with Mr Carver's taxi service in the background. (© Art Shay Archive)

Navigator Robert Timms (third from the left), survivor of the Kassel raid, with the French crew in the Tibenham Greyhound. (KMHS via Linda Dewey)

Now in the hands of the Germans, a very disappointed Lt Nelson Dimick had planned a party in the Tibenham Greyhound: 'At five o'clock this afternoon I would start my twentieth year of existence on planet earth. A couple of days before I had purchased two fifths of very good Scotch, from the officers' club ('black market' booze). I had a date with an English girl, enlisted in the Royal Air Force (*sic*). We had to be careful around the main streets of Norwich. Officers were not allowed to go with enlisted personnel. The Military Police seemed to take great pleasure in harassing us when caught together and we had already been warned a couple of times. However we were not deterred by regulations.' He was going to be extremely late for the party, and the WRAF girl would have to find a new date.

One of the biggest benefits of having an American 'town' in the middle of your village was for the children. The GIs responded generously to pleas from local kids sitting on the gate saying, 'Got any gum, chum?' Kids arrived home with 'K' rations, biscuits (cookies to the Americans) or glucose sweets taken from the escape kits. It was impossible to keep tight security as some properties were within the base and local roads crossed parts of the base as well. Local kids could always find a way into the heart of the airfield, where they were quickly 'adopted' by friendly servicemen plying them with goodies, sneaking into the cinema to watch the latest movies, having tours of the aircraft and, at Christmas, a party was laid on with unheard of luxuries like oranges, ice cream and 'donuts' served to incredulous children who had never seen or tasted them before. There were also presents provided by an American version of Father Christmas.

Eleven-year-old John Wenn had a privileged position as he had an aunt living on Plantation Road, which was now within the base. He had managed to persuade the Provost Marshal to take his photograph and issue a pass with it on, so he could legitimately visit the crew members in hut 14, who had befriended the youngster. He would eat with them on a Saturday, attending the mess with his own set of cutlery. When he left the Christmas party he could barely carry all the presents he had been given.

The Group history records the first Christmas day in the group's new home:

> Christmas Day, 1943, was a memorable day in many respects. There were both Protestant and Catholic religious services for those who wished to attend. Catholic Mass was scheduled for 9 o'clock in the morning in the Base Theater. Quite a number of men arrived several minutes early, and the sight they saw was completely disheartening.
>
> The theater had been used the day before to entertain neighboring British children at a Christmas party. The concrete floor was a mass of overturned benches, pieces of doughnut and other bits of food, and an abundant supply of waste paper. Through lack of coordination, no provision had been made for a detail of men to clean the theater after the party. However, because all were determined to make this first Christmas overseas as pleasant as possible, everyone pitched in to clean up the place before the Chaplain arrived. Both officers and enlisted men wielded brooms which were borrowed from the Mess Hall next door, picked up the larger pieces of paper, righted benches, and in general tried to make the place presentable. The Chaplain finally arrived about 9:30. There was no heat in the theater, and it was distinctly uncomfortable kneeling on the cold concrete in the chilly atmosphere still foggy with the dust that had been stirred up in

the hasty sweeping. But when the Chaplain led the singing of several Christmas carols, the hut resounded with the beloved melodies, which rivaled in quality any choir back in the States that day, even though there was no musical accompaniment. The big attraction in the Mess Halls was our turkey dinners. This time there was plenty of gobbler – no pork – and the trimmings were practically up to home standards.

Christmas packages had been arriving for the past few days, and even on Christmas Day many of the men received the welcome ·boxes from home. It might be added, however, that we continued to receive our Christmas packages right up till the end of March 1944.

(Birsic, Rudolph J., *The history of the 445th Bombardment Group (H)* (unofficial) (1947))

Now some of these same children were standing on the edge of bare hard-stands or sitting on the doorstep of empty huts in floods of tears, many realizing their friends had gone, empty beds with their folded blankets and sheets a testimony to the disaster that had befallen.

Above and opposite above: Christmas party for the local children in the base theatre. (Norfolk Gliding Club archive)

It wasn't only the children who were devastated. Many of the local ladies had American boyfriends, and when the bombers came home they could be seen cycling towards the base. Local girls were invited to the regular dances and others were trucked in from Norwich to hear popular bands and learn how to jitterbug. Glenn Miller performed in one of the T2 hangars once before his untimely death.

The motor pool provided trucks each night to take men on pass to Norwich. Once there, men were on their own, but they had to be back at the Cattle Market at 2200 hours to return to base. On arrival in Norwich men headed to one of the local pubs, unless they had prearranged a meeting with a young lady. The crews usually headed for the city centre – the Bell and Maid's Head hotels and Backs Pub proved popular venues – and Norwich was full of American airmen. The Samson and Hercules and The Lido Dance Halls were popular locations for the jitterbugging 'Yanks' and their consorts to dance. The original Samson and Hercules mansion was built by the Mayor of Norwich, Christopher Jay, in 1657 and the place became a ballroom in 1939. It proved a popular haunt for those stationed at both USAAF and RAF airbases around Norwich, until it was severely damaged by fire in 1944.

Initially bombed in the summer of 1940, Norwich was not attacked again until April and May 1942 as part of the so-called Baedeker raids, in which targets were chosen for their cultural and historical value, not as strategic or military targets, using a series of pre-war tourist guides called the Baedeker guides. The most devastating of these attacks occurred on the evening of 27 April 1942, continuing on 29 April. There were further attacks in May and a heavy bombardment on 26 and 27 June in which Norwich Cathedral was badly damaged. Norwich Castle, City Hall and the Guildhall all escaped, while many residential streets were destroyed. A total of 681 high-explosive bombs claimed the lives of 340 killed and more than 1,000 seriously injured by the summer of 1944. GIs stared in amazement at the bombed-out houses and the boarded-up shop windows as they strolled around the city looking for entertainment.

On their entertainment sorties into Norwich, men who missed the truck departures and did not have an overnight pass were faced with the choice of taking a train to Tivetshall (if the last train south had not left), hire a taxi or,

Norwich was heavily bombed in the war. (Norwich Library archives)

if they were from one of the closer bases, travelling by bicycle. On the narrow, blacked-out roads, perhaps with more than a few beers on board, it could be quite a risky trip back and quite a few wound up in the ditches – and sometimes hospital! For those with longer passes – usually three days or sometimes a week – and who could afford the time and money to travel further, there were the delights of London with its bars, nightclubs and nude revues at the famous Windmill Theatre among the main attractions. There was also the seamier side of London with the famous 'Piccadilly Commandos' (hookers) offering their services at inflated prices to the wealthy American clientele.

Some of the Americans' imported 'ladies' remained hidden on the base for several days, and managed to avoid the 'Snowdrops' (military police) searching for them by moving from hut to hut, offering their wares, until they were rounded up and shipped out. Some girlfriends were smuggled onto aircraft on training flights and a few crewmembers wound up joining the 'mile high club' in the fuselage of the vibrating bombers using yellow dinghy packs as cushions.

With an overall death rate of 7.2 per cent, an American bomber over Europe was the most dangerous place to be, even beating the Marines

The attractions and distractions of wartime London were easier for those on American pay. (© Art Shay Archive)

engaged in the bloody struggle for the Japanese-held islands in the Pacific. So life had to be lived, and moments were stolen whenever possible.

The British had a much more tolerant attitude to coloured Americans than the US army, who still maintained a segregation policy, even though many Brits – particularly in rural areas – had never seen a Negro until the war started. The different attitudes caused considerable trouble on several occasions with both the civil and military police being called to fights, usually at local pubs and dance halls. At one pub a compromise was reached with separate nights allocated to black and white troops.

Lt Robert Toeppe, navigator on a visit to London with some members of his crew displayed some of the attitudes at the time in this extract from his diary:

> Pete, Vaughn, Orland (Lt Orland H. Hasselbach), Mathews (Lt C.A. Matthews) and I went to London on the ten o'clock train. We were greeted by a couple of 'commandos' and we went to dinner with them. Pete and Vaughn took over and we went over to the Reindeer Club where we stayed. When we were having dinner a Negro soldier walked in with an English woman and her son. We got so damned mad we walked out. The English (women) go out with the Negroes here and seem to prefer them to the white men. Of course this isn't a general habit. When the Negroes first came over, they passed as American Indians, the dirty rats. We walked around and couldn't get in a movie and we finally had dinner at the Regent Palace, it was very nice. We had a long talk with a couple of English girls who had visited the United States. It was very interesting. Orland and I walked about Piccadilly Circus and Oxford Circus. It was very interesting and it's true what they say about Piccadilly.

The military police on the base were also kept busy, recovering stolen vehicles and bikes, guarding prisoners and crashed aircraft, as the report opposite for the month of April shows:

Stratford-upon-Avon and Scotland also proved popular to those who wished to see more of the 'Old Country' rather than the grimy, soot-stained, foggy streets of the capital.

BACK AT BASE

During the month regular Military Police and Interior Guard duties were performed, with seven posts and continuous patrol. These included the following:

Additional guards were furnished one new plane and two crashed planes on the base.

Guards for a total of 202 hours duty furnished on two crashed planes off the base.

On five "Action Stations" alerts and one practice alert, guards were doubled and mobile reserve platoon formed.

Eighteen blackout violations were reported.

Four vehicles accidents were reported on the station.

One civilian and US vehicle accident on highway 2 miles west of the station was investigated and a report made to 2d Air Division.

Thirteen Enlisted Men were reported for violations of Bicycle Regulations.

Spot check made daily of civilian gas lorries for retained gas.

Thirteen jeeps and two command cars were reported stolen on the base and recovered by the Military Police.

Eighty nine bicycles reported stolen and 83 were recovred.

MPs supervised base trash details and policing daily.

Two Enlisted Men were reported for uniform violations off the station.

Military Police Report. (Norfolk gliding club archive)

Back to War

Despite the disastrous raid, the base had to continue operating, and word came through that another mission was going to Kassel the following day. Ground crews worked through the night to get enough aircraft serviceable out of the twenty-six Liberators left on the base and eventually ten were scraped together to fly. Captain Web Uebelhoer, the surviving deputy leader, was asked if he would lead the mission and this time his reply was, 'Thanks, but no thanks.'

Back from leave, Chuck Walker went to briefing the next day and, when the curtain was pulled back there was a stunned silence as the red line went back to Kassel. Ten Liberators led by Captain Rowe Bowen joined in with the 389th Bomber Group and flew to bomb Kassel – this time without loss!

The only crew scheduled to fly, who had been rostered on the previous day, was that of 1st Lt Rene Schneider, who hadn't managed to get off the ground when he cut a tyre and aborted. Now he knew the disaster he had narrowly avoided, it took a special kind of courage to fly the second mission to Kassel.

In all, the 445th managed to put ten aircraft in the air on the 28th – and they all bombed the original Kassel target and returned safely.

Lieutenant Glen Lowe of the 702nd Squadron was waiting for transport back to the Zone of Interior (ZOI) as he had finished his tour earlier in September. His original bombardier, Lt Ira Weinstein, was now a PoW, having gone down with the Donald crew in *Flossye*. Glen helped to sanitize the lives of the missing airmen. As the personal belongings were sent back to the States, the custom was to sort through them so nothing embarrassing, such as a married man's letters from a British girlfriend, or indelicate items like condoms, would go home.

For the cleaning parties, all those who were not back on the base were counted as MIA (missing in action), so as the crews who had managed

Some of the heavy damage inflicted on Kassel on 27 September and other subsequent raids. Photo taken 29 April 1945. (NARA)

The Henschel Tank factory badly damaged. (NARA)

These almost completed locomotives never hauled supplies to German lines, for Henschel's plants were ruined by bombing. In nineteen attacks during 1944-45, the 8th AF and the RAF aimed 10,975 tons of bombs on Kassel targets. (NARA)

to land at Manston or crash-land in Allied territory made their way back to Tibenham, they found their belongings being sorted through and their bunks stacked with their bedding neatly folded. The kit of the missing was packed up, and collected, apart from some of the personal effects, taken by friends or redistributed – everybody on the base ended up with a new bike!

In Lt John French's hut, their ex-bombardier, Claude Switzer, refused to believe his former crew was dead and when the quartermaster sergeant turned up to collect their belongings he refused to let him in the hut. He defied a lieutenant on the same errand, and by the time the Major arrived he had calmed down and the belongings scattered and hidden. His belief turned out well-founded, because at around that time his crewmates were drinking Scotch and sodas in a French chateau, and on their return to Tibenham next day they were grateful to get all their belongings back.

Some survivors let off a little steam at the new crews who were quickly dispatched to rebuild the 445th. Web Uebelhoer's navigator, Lieutenant Donald Whitefield, put on his Colt 45 and steel helmet to give them a real serious scenario of how rough things were.

Assembly of Prisoners

Meanwhile back in Germany, most of those who were still trying to evade the searching forces had hidden away in the woods and farms surrounding the crash sites. Those already picked up were being brought together in various locations and, over the next few days, other captured airmen joined them.

Frank Bertram woke after a cold night in the forest under the hunter's lookout and started to make his way across country through dense woodland when he heard movement. He threw away his pistol, so he wasn't armed if captured, only to come face to face with a large stag with an impressive set of antlers. Probably as scared as Frank, it took off, crashing through the undergrowth. Frank started following the Werra River, while still able to stay on the edge of the woods, and came across a small field of potatoes where he stopped to fill his pockets before continuing his journey. He had to avoid a group of men working on the wreckage of the downed Liberator of Captain Chilton and then walked out into a beautiful valley in more open country. He couldn't move quickly as he had to use a stick for support, and was trying to cross the valley when he saw a group of youths out collecting propaganda leaflets which had been dropped in the area. Frank tried to hide behind a tree on the edge of a creek when a 12-year-old, Walter Hassenpflug, spotted him. The German youngster ran off, but returned with other members of the Hitler youth, one of whom could speak a little English and offered some assistance to the injured airman. They helped him up from the edge of the creek, then across a bridge and into the local village, where they met a couple of policemen, who took Frank into custody. They put him in a solitary cell, searched him and removed his wallet and lucky charm baseball mitt before leaving him alone. He was resting on a straw-covered plank which acted as a bed, when two English officers, recaptured escapees from a German PoW camp, made contact. The officers had had their escape provisions of cocoa, cheese, crackers and sugar returned to them by the Germans and they decided to pass what they couldn't consume onto Frank. The remainder was later confiscated by the guards, who came to collect the English prisoners, but they had already shared the provisions not only with a very hungry Frank but also the German guard. Frank had stuffed his pockets with the leftovers.

Later that night the cell door flew open and a young woman, who had been present when he had arrived at the jail, returned his good-luck charm baseball mitt and prayer book. Early the next day he was transported by car to the local Luftwaffe camp, which now held about fifteen of the captured airmen, including Corman Bean and Eugene George. The Germans were now collecting the captives into larger groups for transportation to the Dulag Luft prison at Oberursel near Frankfurt-am-Main. It was being used as a clearing station for captured airmen, who were processed and interrogated before shipment to various prison camps. Frank's group was escorted to the local railway station where they met about thirty-five other guys, including a beaten-up George Collar who had two black eyes and a broken nose, and little Ira Weinstein. The rest were an assortment of airmen in various states of discomfort: some had no shoes, others had broken bones, and nearly all were black and blue with bruises and hungry, as most hadn't eaten since breakfast at Tibenham the previous day. Frank emptied his pockets of the supplies left over from the English officers and shared them with his fellow prisoners. Later all fifty were loaded onto a train heading for Frankfurt and Oberursel. While this battered band of brothers was being transported by rail, the search continued for others still on the run.

One of those still on the loose was gunner S/Sgt Glen McCormick. After bailing out of Captain Chilton's lead ship, he had delayed his parachute opening until after he had fallen through the cloud layer, pulled the ripcord and, with a jolt, found himself descending towards woods and fields when he was greeted by a couple of P51 Mustangs as they went past waggling their wings. He landed in a tree, but managed to climb down undetected and set off to hide in the woods until dark. He found a hunters' shooting hide and settled down for several hours wait. He was disturbed by a youth, who ran off, and Glen decided to move on. He was on the run for several days, but as he was crossing a clearing he was spotted by a German soldier and a farm worker, who captured him and took him by horse and cart to the local Burgomeister. He was held in the local jail where he met another 445th crew member, and the next day the pair were taken to the railway station and escorted to the local Luftwaffe airbase and on to Frankfurt to join up with the others at the Oberursel interrogation centre. Having endured the mixture of bribes and threats he (along with several others – including two more members of the same crew) was escorted to the train by two elderly soldiers.

Passenger trains and those with prisoners had the lowest priority and several times they were sidelined for hours. Guards would go to get their canteens filled with beer, and occasionally they would share it with the prisoners and a friendly rapport built up. The German beer was a lager type and was more like the drink the Americans were used to 'back home'. They preferred it to the warm dark-mild or bitter beers the English served in their pubs.

Eventually, after several beer stops, some slightly-inebriated guards discharged their captives at Gross Tychow, Luft IV Camp.

Second Lt William Flickner, navigator in *Fridget Bridget*, and 1st Lt Richard Fromm, pilot of H model B-24 080, had been on the run for a week, surviving mainly on a diet of apples and berries. The pair had travelled about twenty-five miles south-west to the village of Nenterode where they walked into a Landwacht patrol composed mostly of elderly first-world-war veterans. The patrol had been attracted to a house by the sound of barking dogs when they saw the two Americans and challenged them. The airmen gave up without any resistance. On the way to the village of Rengshausen, where there was an empty cell to put them in at the juvenile correctional facility, they met the English-speaking manager Georg Noble, who started to interview the two fliers. He got no reply from Richard Fromm and turned to William Flickner to see whether he could get any answers from him. Richard used the lack of attention on him as an opportunity to escape and, despite an intensive search of the area, the Landwacht weren't able to find him. This probably saved his life.

The unresisting William was put in the Beiser-haus detention cell for the night and in the morning was collected by a 52-year-old policeman, Johannes Gremmler, who took him in the direction of Ersrode. There were no witnesses to the next events, so it's a mystery what happened, but William was shot in the back five times by Gremmler 'while trying to escape' and became the 117th and final casualty. Gremmler was arrested after the war but committed suicide before his trial.

Richard Fromm continued to evade capture and was on the run until Saturday, 21 October, but after twenty-four days the weakened and very hungry pilot was finally captured by a civilian armed with a hunting rifle in a wood near Lembach. He was handed over to local policeman Sergeant Walter, who turned out to be more humane than Gremmler. Richard was handed over to the Luftwaffe unharmed and started his journey to a PoW camp as the 121st and last 445th airman captured. A total of 117 airmen had died – 114 in Germany and one each in France, Belgium and England.

After a few days in the cells, lying on wooden benches in the basement and surviving on a diet of barley porridge for breakfast, a piece of black bread and cup of ersatz acorn coffee for dinner, they were interrogated, with little success.

Apart from losing his government-issue watch, being hungry and tired, George Collar was unharmed, among a group of approximately twenty-five guys assembled at the train station to be transported to an air-base at Erfurt. They were guarded by two Luftwaffe sergeants armed with sub-machine guns, and warned by the guards to keep a low profile. They were also ordered to secrete loaves of bread for the journey under the blankets of the stretcher-borne wounded, and to keep the bread out of sight of local civilians. The airmen were loaded into a railcar and the train set off.

When they reached Erfurt it was a hot, sunny day, and they had to march while carrying the stretchers. Exhausted and dehydrated, they finally stopped for a break, when they were shown some kindness by being given water by a German lady. They tried to use a handcart to carry the wounded until a puncture ended that method of transport and carrying had to be resumed. It was early evening before they managed to stagger exhausted into the Luftwaffe hospital in Erfurt. Not having to carry a stretcher because of his difficulty in walking, Mac MacGregor was limping along with this group for treatment on his legs. When he reached the hospital Mac was perturbed by the sight of an attractive nurse who's apron was covered in blood and clutching an instrument for digging out shrapnel. Fortunately the doctor explained to a worried Mac that they could take out all the shrapnel but he would probably live with no trouble with it left alone.

They were incarcerated there for two days, fed only meagre rations in the freezing cells, and then the dispirited group of airmen lined up again and were loaded into a truck and driven back to Erfurt railway station, where they were assembled in the station waiting to board a train to Frankfurt-am-Main. While waiting, they were accosted by a couple of SS soldiers who started to work up passing civilians into a mob intent on revenge on the 'terrorfliegers'. It was just starting to get nasty when a Luftwaffe colonel arrived and proceeded to read the riot act to the soldiers and the assembled crowd, who quickly dispersed. With relief, the prisoners boarded the train, which soon pulled out of Erfurt and set off for Frankfurt. It arrived late at night in the badly-damaged and glass-littered station, which had previously been the scene of the lynching of captured Allied airmen.

The prisoners' railcar was parked in the sidings and the engine left. After a while another crowd started to gather hurling bricks and abuse at the PoWs. It was only the guards threatening to use their machine pistols which prevented further bloodshed. They were assisted by an air-raid warning, which caused the crowd to disperse quickly for shelter.

After the all-clear sounded a locomotive arrived, hooked up the carriages and, puffing large quantities of white steam, continued the journey to Oberursel interrogation centre.

It was very late at night when the airmen were marched from the station to the centre, and the guards, unsure of the route, had to get directions from locals. But eventually the gang of weary airmen arrived at the camp courtyard to find it full of British and Polish paratroopers who had recently been captured in the Arnhem 'bridge too far' debacle. The group was split up for another night in various cells and the following morning they were fed cabbage soup, which to the starving Americans actually tasted quite good. They were kept in the cells for a couple of days with the temperature alternating between extremely hot and freezing, which was probably a deliberate policy to lower morale and soften up the by now cold, dejected prisoners. Then they were taken one at a time for interrogation.

Most of the aircrew had seen the film about 'Resisting Enemy Interrogation' on arrival in the ETO and had been told repeatedly not to divulge anything but name, rank and serial number and not to try to outsmart the German interrogator or get involved in a conversation.

After a mixture of bribes, cigarettes, drinks and the offer of letting family know they were safe by filling in fake Red Cross forms, if interrogators failed to elicit any response other than name, rank and number, then the interrogation soon took on a different tone, with threats of violence, being turned over to the Gestapo as a spy, or spells in solitary confinement.

Nearly all American PoWs transiting through the Oberursel detention centre were amazed at the amount of information the Germans already had on them. Interrogation officers could often quote the group, squadron, and names of the commanding officers, names and addresses of family members and sometimes even where the unfortunate prisoner had worked. This was designed to make the prisoner feel that since the Germans already knew so much about them, it hardly mattered to indulge in idle chit chat. Some prisoners fell for it and unwittingly gave away snippets of information which the Germans meticulously recorded and used to build a picture of what was going on back on the Allies' side.

With a few exceptions, most of the captured 445th aircrew where now incarcerated at Oberursel. One morning, along with some paratroopers from Arnhem and a mixture of other aircrews, they were assembled in the courtyard and ordered to remove their shoes, tie the laces together and pile them on blankets as a deterrent to escaping. George Collar hoped this would lead to him being able to get a better pair! Unfortunately that didn't happen when the shoes were returned.

After a few days of fruitless interrogation, the Germans usually gave up and shipped out batches of prisoners. Ira Weinstein, who was in the next group to leave, had managed to hang onto the watch given to him by his family before he was sent overseas. Before leaving, his group was processed for departure. Their clothes were taken away to be deloused and, as they were sent for a shower, Ira met a New Zealand prisoner who told him the Germans were confiscating everything. So, reluctantly, he handed the Kiwi his treasured Longines Aviator watch. He never expected to see it again but at least he had the satisfaction that a German wasn't going to benefit from it.

The Germans brought out the blankets full of shoes and the prisoners retrieved their own before they were marched to the railway station for shipment to the Luftwaffe-controlled camp at Dulag Luft Wetzlar. While waiting in the sidings, Ira spotted the man he had given his watch to in the train alongside his. The New Zealander managed to throw the precious timepiece back to an very surprised and lucky Ira Weinstein.

By this stage of the war it was extremely dangerous to travel by rail in daylight as fighters on their way home from escorting bombers had been given permission to descend to low level to strafe anything of value as a target. Railway engines giving out clouds of steam were easily spotted and became sitting ducks for the marauding Thunderbolts, Mustangs and Lightnings.

To avoid being strafed, the train had to hide in tunnels when it could, but eventually reached the station at Wetzlar. The prisoners had just disembarked when a couple of P51s appeared and George Collar, among others, thought that they were going to be attacked and become victims of 'friendly fire'. Maybe the Mustang pilots recognized that the troops on the ramp were PoWs, or they were low on fuel or ammunition, but they didn't strafe the train or station and flew off to the north-west, probably heading home for a date back at their base. The relieved prisoners were marched up to a holding camp where they were kept for a few days before being shipped in batches to their final camp.

Reg Miner was put in a passenger carriage, which was a distinct improvement on the usual mode of German rail transport for prisoners – a cattle truck or boxcar with a bucket for sanitary arrangements. On this occasion, however, ten men were crammed into a carriage designed for six, so turns had to be taken to sleep on the baggage racks or floor while the others slouched in their seats. The journey took four days through a heavily-damaged Berlin and onto Stalag Luft 1, near Barth, on the Baltic coast in northern Germany.

The camp contained mainly aircrew, with 12,000 American, British and Canadian prisoners. Stalag Luft had two compounds with a third under construction. North One had its own mess hall but North Two did not have a mess hall and the prisoners took turns to cook on the stove in their room. There were sixteen prisoners to a 24 x 16ft room with about ten rooms to a building, which was elevated to allow the 'goons' – as the German guards were known – to search for tunnels easily.

On arrival at Barth, and other camps, many of the airmen were greeted by buddies or relatives already there, having been 'invited to the party' when they were shot down by Germans on earlier missions. Several familiar faces greeted the latest marching column of aircrew as they arrived and Ira Weinstein walked through the prison compound gate to be greeted by his brother-in-law, shot down six weeks earlier.

Prisoners had double bunks to start with but, later, a third tier was added. Mac McGregor was put up on the third tier and was by now feeling so weak on the nearly starvation diet that, when he got out of bed,

Prisoners-of-war arriving at the station in Barth. (Courtesy of Heinrich Haslob – German guard)

Mac MacGregor's PoW ID Card. (Courtesy of his daughter, Mona English)

South compound, Stalag Luft 1, Barth. (Norfolk Gliding Club archive)

he often felt faint and had to hang on to the bed post to stop himself falling from the top tier.

Ira Weinstein, like all the new arrivals, settled down to a cold, hungry existence, brightened occasionally by the issue of Red Cross parcels, the mainstay of the PoW diet. The rest of their meals consisted of thin, watery cabbage soup, a small piece of black bread, the occasional potato and, sometimes, a piece of rancid meat in the soup.

Red Cross parcels, which came in cardboard boxes, were a godsend to prisoners and included: a tin of Klim (milk spelt backwards!) powdered milk; cookies; margarine; sugar; cheese; a tin of coffee; chocolate D-Bars; Jam; fifty cigarettes; tins of sardines or salmon; Spam; and soap and toilet paper. The parcels were normally issued at the rate of one parcel between two men once a week – but that could easily stretch to ten days.

The Germans often used the parcels as bargaining chips and their issue could be erratic depending on how the war was going and the prisoners' behaviour. Once no parcels were distributed for nearly two months and that caused starvation and illness among the PoWs. It wasn't unusual for parcels to be pillaged by the guards, with the cans of coffee or cigarettes missing when they were issued.

Lt Palmer Bruland, at Stalag 1, passed the time using a razor blade to engrave the names of the men living in his barracks, along with the beautifully-carved wings of a bald eagle. The single razor blade had turned up in a Red Cross parcel. Palmer eventually collected enough cigarettes and chocolate bars to trade with the German guard for a little pocket knife. He was then able to carve a B-24 Liberator with four rotating propellers, but it was too fragile to take when he was liberated. He did however manage to retain his book of poetry and drawings made from Red cross wrappers.

Empty tins were turned into all sorts of equipment, ranging from simple cups and plates, to an eggbeater which Ira Weinstein took back to the USA on his release in 1945.

But days passed slowly for the PoWs, who spent their time reading, playing games – also supplied by the Red Cross – or doing household chores, like cooking for the hut which had to be done on a small stove with a very limited supply of fuel. That was no mean feat for a hut of about twenty-four very hungry guys. Those at Barth fared better than in other camps as they usually got a Red Cross parcel – along with a shower – once a week, until the later months of the war. The Kassel raid survivors only had seven months as prisoners before they were liberated and were in better condition

Above and below: Extracts from Palmer Bruland's book. (Courtesy Cathy and Peter Barton)

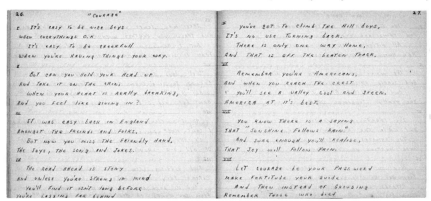

than the bulk of inmates, but George Collar still lost a fifth of his weight, down to 135lbs from 170, by the time liberation came.

With the northern latitude and the wind coming straight off the Baltic Sea, the winter months were extremely cold, and standing outside for roll call, sometimes for hours at a time, was a feat of endurance.

The war ground on slowly and, after the failure of the Battle of the Bulge and the steady advance of the Russians, it became obvious to the German authorities that the camp wouldn't be tenable for much longer, and plans were put in place for its liquidation. The South compound was emptied first and the prisoners transferred to the North, then most of the Jewish inmates were rounded up and put together in the South compound. Somehow Ira Weinstein was missed in this round up, although his brother-in-law and several friends were forced to go. Ira spoke to the senior American officer in the camp, fighter ace Col Hubert Zemke, but he was told to shut up and keep quiet as he didn't know how lucky he had been. Chastened, Ira returned to his hut wondering why. The Flak school close to the camp started to blow up everything that was of any use and shrapnel from the explosions forced inmates to take cover in the slit trenches they had been allowed to dig earlier.

Col Zemke was a fighter ace with more than seventeen kills to his name. He wound up as a 'guest' of the Luftwaffe after losing a wing of his P51 Mustang in extreme turbulence over Germany in early November 1944. As senior Allied officer of the camp he steadily developed a relationship with the new commandant, Oberst Warnstadt, and managed to improve conditions and protect his charges. As the Red Army approached, he not only negotiated to prevent the massacre of the Jewish prisoners in the South compound, which had been ordered by Himmler, but also refused to march all the prisoners to the west as other eastern PoW camps were doing. Instead he negotiated that the German guards would vacate the camp, leaving the prisoners behind to greet the Russians. On the morning of 30 April, the inmates woke to find themselves alone in the camp as the Germans had secretly moved out overnight. The next day the first Russian soldier – a drunken officer riding a white horse – arrived. The first Russian troops to arrive were front-line troops who were mainly well-disciplined and more interested in getting the war finished, but the support troops following consisted mainly of a rabble intent on taking revenge on the local populace by raping, looting and killing. The local jeweller was shot and his store looted, along with several others, and soldiers ran about with arms full of looted wristwatches and drunk from brandy looted from a ship's cargo they had found.

The Burgomeister of Barth shot his whole family and then himself to avoid falling into their hands.

Second Lt Edmund F. Boomhower, navigator from the Golden crew in *Old Baldy*, recorded the day's event on a scrap of paper:-

> Blk. 7, Rm. 3, North #3
> Stalag Luft I
> Tuesday Morning, May 1, 1945 –
>
> I wake up, or should I say I am awakened by my fellow kriegie sleeping next to me, and look out of the barracks window in the direction of the guard tower and what do I see – an AMERICAN INSTEAD OF A GERMAN standing there. It is only 5 o'clock and therefore barely light outside, which makes it difficult to see – but Germans don't wear B-10 jackets with white arm bands. There are also Americans patrolling the OUTSIDE of the fence. The Americans are now in control of the camp! It hardly seems possible after waiting so long now that it's actually here, that we have only to wait until Joe gets here to go home...home to all those things we have dreamed of and missed so much, after having been, by turns, optimistic and then pessimistic. It just doesn't seem conceivable – our minds can't grasp it – we are all in a sort of daze – it's too good to be true. But it is true! Shortly we will again see face to face our loved ones. We will be back to the good old U.S.A. under those beautiful Stars and Stripes...Oh say, can you see...? We see the homes we left behind, our wives and mothers, brothers, sisters, fathers, sweethearts, and friends. And that's not all – we see ourselves, us, you & I in those homes in those United States! God grant that we may never have to leave again.... Amen.
>
> 10:23 pm May 1, 1945 – THE RUSSIANS ARE HERE!!!
>
> (Courtesy of Tim Boomhower)

The Russians treated the PoWs (who wore black armbands to denote their status) with some respect. Col Zemke had great difficulty keeping the Americans confined to camp, with many going on escapades in the local town, and some 3-400 who couldn't wait for evacuation made their own way westwards. Some followed in the wake of the advancing Russian forces, managed to get through to the British lines and were evacuated to

Brussels where they were put up in a five-star hotel – an extreme difference to their lifestyle a few days earlier! The remaining inmates in the camp were glad to get away from the Russians when some B17s arrived to start evacuation to Le Havre and Camp Lucky Strike.

T/Sgt Howard Boldt, gunner from Lt Baynham's *King Kong*, wounded by three-inch pieces of shrapnel and with very badly broken legs, was in hospital at Obermassfeld, near the railway at Meiningen. He was in a plaster cast, unable to get up for five months, and life was a never-ending round of injections and pain, with serious infections causing boils and bedsores from his inactivity. But Howard eventually had the cast removed and was able to start to get about on crutches, which proved very useful as the hospital was nearly strafed by marauding Mustangs. About half-a-dozen of the P51s attacked two trains in the station after pulling up just over the hospital and then strafing. One P51 was hit by a small flak gun mounted on the back of one of the trains and it crashed in a fireball, the other 51s exacted revenge for their buddy's loss by strafing the flat-car, killing the gunners. They came close to the hospital when they made several more passes on the trains and inflicted heavy damage. Howard stayed in the hospital until the advancing 11th Armoured Division of the American army relieved it in early April.

The first American soldiers brought 'K' Rations, which provided a welcome change to the inmates' diet. Breaking into the local dairy also provided fresh milk. Howard and fellow crewmember gunner S/Sgt John Knox were loaded into trucks, along with the other patients, and transferred to division headquarters. They were now safely back in the care of the American army.

Unlike the inmates of Barth camp and the hospital, other prisoners weren't so lucky as to be relieved by the advancing Allied armies. They were forced instead to march westwards away from the advancing Russian army.

Glen McCormick left prison camp Stalag XIII, near Nuremberg, in early April 1945 in a column numbering more than 8,000. They were forced to march westwards. They walked during the day and stopped at night in various farm buildings and barns or camped out in the bitter cold and rain in woods along the way. The column was being followed by SS troops to prevent escape attempts. After marching nearly 100 miles, Glen arrived at prison camp Stalag VII more than a week later, ironically having travelled to Moosberg near Gottingen which the 445th had bombed in error instead of Kassel and close to where he had been shot down in the first place. The American army's 14th Armoured Division liberated the camp, which housed nearly 80,000 prisoners of all nationalities, on 29 April, just before the end of the war. The camp was evacuated by C-47s initially to Reims, where the US airmen were showered, reclothed, fed and rested, before moving on to Camp Lucky Strike, near Le Havre, to meet up with buddies from other camps and to be slowly brought back to their original weights. Their shrunken stomachs couldn't digest food easily and some, especially the long-term prisoners, made themselves seriously ill by gorging on food their digestive systems couldn't cope with.

Another march westwards started from Stalag Luft 4, a camp containing more than 10,000 captives from forty-eight different nations, including *Fort Worth Maid*'s radio operator Charles Graham, wounded tail-gunner Ammi Miller, and from Lt Pearson's ship the radio operator Doyle O'Keefe. Cold and hungry, Charles trudged off across the frozen ground along with thousands of others, while Ammi, unable to walk, fared slightly better in that he was evacuated by train. Again Doyle O'Keefe's army experience made him better equipped than most to survive the continuous marches. His column of about 2,500 prisoners was, as the Allied armies closed in, marched back and forth across Poland and Germany from 7 February until 26 April. Doyle had equipped himself – by a combination of issue, barter and theft – with long underwear, shoelaces to tie up his cuffs and trouser legs to keep out the cold, and lots of pairs of socks. Eventually down to about 250 men, the filthy, louse-infested, starving PoWs persuaded the elderly German guards to surrender their weapons to them, marched westwards over the Elbe river and met up with the US 104th Infantry Brigade and were then cleaned up, issued with new clothes, and fed to the point of bursting before being transported to camp Lucky Strike and the start of the long journey home.

The column Charles was in also camped in barns and fields and had to endure nights out in freezing conditions and lack of food as the Red Cross parcels they had set out with ran out. Several prisoners died on the long-haul 'death march' to the river Elbe. Their desperate situation was made worse by being strafed by 'friendly fire' from marauding Mustangs, and the luckless Charles was slightly wounded in one of these raids. Squeezed between the advancing Russians from the East and the Americans and British from the West, the column marched back and forth until they were finally liberated by General Montgomery's British forces. Charles, who had lost more than 30lbs, was taken to hospital and fed on a diet which included Champagne and milkshakes, neither of which did his digestion much good. He was eventually evacuated to Camp Lucky strike and then shipped home to the USA.

The survivors of the 445th from the different camps, along with all the other liberated PoWs, were usually processed through the 'Cigarette camps', named after famous brands. Lucky Strike was the biggest of these with more than 12,000 tents, complete with hospitals, post exchange, theatre and shops. After processing, the released PoWs waited for shipment from the recently reopened port of Le Havre, either to travel back to the UK or straight to the USA. Some ex-prisoners had to wait weeks, others just a few days, but most were safely back in the arms of their loved ones by early June. Some expected to be remustered and sent to the Far East to fight the Japanese, only the atomic bombs dropped on Japan put an end to the war before they got there.

Of the thirty-nine aircraft scheduled to fly at Tibenham that fateful September morning:
One never got off the ground
Two aborted and returned to Tibenham
One aborted and landed on the continent
Twenty-five were shot down in Germany
One crash-landed in Belgium
Two crashed or crash-landed in France
Two landed, badly damaged, at Manston on the English coast
One crashed at Old Buckenham in Norfolk
Four returned to Tibenham

Of the 370 guys scheduled to fly that day:
9 never left Tibenham
18 returned to Tibenham due to aborts
117 were killed, with a least eight – and possibly 11 – murdered by the Germans
121 were PoWs or on the run
42 landed back at Tibenham
63 landed elsewhere and were making their way home. Some arrived that night, others took more than a week to return to duty.

Which meant there were only sixty-nine for supper that evening, while over one hundred of their friends where lying dead, battered and burnt in the German countryside

After the group had managed to put up the heroic ten-aircraft squadron the day after Kassel, attached as high right squadron to the 389th bomber group from Hethel, replacement crews and aircraft arrived quickly and by 2 October the 445th sent twenty aircraft to attack Hamm. The following day it was back up to strength and sent thirty aircraft to Lachen where they recorded excellent bombing results with no losses on either mission.

The war was winding down, but between the Kassel raid on 27 September 1944 and April 1945 the 445th flew another 111 missions and lost another eighteen crews shot down. On 1 April 1945 Lt Bruce Kilborn and his crew in *Axis Ex-Lax* became the last crew lost by the group. Only two gunners and the radar counter-measures crewmen survived and Bruce and six members of his crew were the last airmen to be killed in action flying from Tibenham.

The final mission was flown to Salzburg in Austria on 25 April 1945. Then suddenly it was all over! On 7 May 7 it was announced that the war in Europe had ended and with that the party started. Tracers, mortars and flares filled the air; it was suddenly like the 4th of July independence celebrations. When the party had died down and the hangovers had eased, the 445th settled down to a peacetime routine, flying ground personnel on 'trolley' missions over the German cities at low altitude, so they could see the destruction inflicted on the Third Reich, and resupply missions to help feed the starving Dutch population.

The two aircraft which landed at Manston, Lt Mercer's 42-51549 and Lt Dewey's 42-50855, were repaired and eventually returned to Tibenham. Neither would survive the war and were lost with other crews.

None of the three which crash-landed in France and Belgium returned to Tibenham and were salvaged where they lay.

Afterword

On 17 May 1945 the group received orders to get ready to return to the USA. Events moved quickly, with serviceable aircraft departing daily for the US carrying up to twenty passengers and crew while the ground troops cleared up. They dug pits to bury the contents of buildings and lorries left the base taking more spares and equipment away to larger dumps at Rushall and the sand pits at Flixton. The Flixton pits had provided much of the sand and gravel for constructing the miles of concrete at Tibenham and all the other bases which formed the 'Fields of Little America'.

Rather than sell the hard-come-by and expensive bicycles the astute Fred Dodger and others had overcharged them for (and who were now offering just a few shillings for bikes which had cost several pounds a few months earlier), guys took the matter into their own hands. Fire axes were used to smash some and, determined that locals weren't going to benefit when they left, some bikes were put on the main runway and driven over by the small caterpillar 'dozers' used to pull the bomb trains and aircraft through the mud. The bent bicycle frames were then buried in the bomb dump. Others gave their bikes away. Local boy John Wenn awoke one morning to find a dozen bikes left in the garden with a message wishing him 'goodbye' scrawled on the path with a stone. The big clean-up continued apace until the early hours of 28 May.

When the lorries with the remaining Americans departed Tibenham for the last time, they left a trail of broken hearts, one or two pregnancies, and a sudden gap in the locals' lives. The area became eerily quiet. There was no longer the roar of Pratt and Whitney engines or the noise of traffic bringing in men and material. The pubs were suddenly empty and the airfield looked like a ghost town. Many people were devastated and it took a while for the community to recover – not only from the loss of friends, but also the economic impact. Washing no longer needed doing, workers on the base lost their jobs, and the shops and pubs lost trade.

The bulk of the 445th had left. Those who hadn't managed to get a ride home by air travelled by lorry to Bristol docks, except for 703rd Squadron personnel who were shipped to Southampton. But both groups boarded small US army transports for the journey home – a big change for those who had shipped over on the big Queen liners some twenty months earlier.

The ships docked at Staten Island after the ten-day crossing home and the two groups met up at Camp Kilmer. They were then sent home for leave before being disbanded at Fort Dix on 12 September 1945. They arrived home to mixed receptions. Some were met by huge crowds, photographed by the local press, and attended big celebratory parties, others quietly got off the train or bus and had to walk back to their homes alone. Sgt Alvis Kitchen's family hadn't had a notification that he was a PoW and thought he was dead, until his father happened to be driving past the railway station and recognized his son disembarking from the train.

Most of the men were demobbed and returned to their civilian jobs. Others stayed in the Air Force as a career, while some took advantage of the government's scheme to take college courses and retrain. After the life-changing events they had been through, readjusting to civilian life didn't come easily but, in the case of most of the PoWs, the large amount of back pay they had accumulated while in the camps helped. The cash funded deposits on a new home or the purchase of a car, a holiday in the sun or parties with wives or girlfriends to make up for lost time.

Some shipped GI brides over from the UK. One or two moved back to Britain to live with their new-found families.

For the men of the 445th, that was it. It was all over. Some visited the families of their crew members who hadn't come back, with mixed receptions between hostility that they had survived while their sons hadn't, to others grateful for the information on the loss of their loved one. Others just didn't want to talk about it and got on with rebuilding their lives. Later some would rekindle their interest and join the 2nd Air Division Association, attending reunions in the USA, UK and Germany, meeting up with old crew mates and even one-time enemies, to reminisce their past encounters.

For a little while the RAF used Tibenham's runways, mainly for landing Lancaster bombers flying on Operation *Dodge*, repatriating ex-PoWs from Germany and Italy. Then in August 1945 Tibenham aerodrome was just put into 'care and maintenance' and left.

The local council took over some and altered a few of the now-empty Nissen huts, dividing the buildings up to make small bedrooms and a living area with a primitive kitchen and bathroom. The huts were used as temporary homes for bombed-out families until proper council houses could be provided.

The airfield lay almost derelict for nearly ten years, with just an occasional maintenance man on site, but the clear-up slowly continued. A couple of old fuselages, which had been used as 'Hangar Queens', were taken away to join the huge pile of wrecked aircraft from all nations behind the Half Moon pub in Rushall, seven miles away, known locally as 'Aluminum Alley'. Their removal deprived local kids of one of their playgrounds! The wind blew through the empty huts and hangars, doors swung and creaked in the breeze, almost like a ghost town in a Hollywood cowboy movie.

The airfield slowly fell into disrepair, with pilferage and vandalism taking its toll. Glass was smashed, whole buildings disappeared and doors and window frames were stolen until, in 1955, the airfield was given a new lease of life.

The cold war was heating up, the Russian Bear was exercising its claws and the UK had started to use 'V' bombers as its main nuclear defence. Tibenham was listed as a base for the big bombers, so the main runway was lengthened and strengthened with another foot of concrete and a layer of asphalt on top of the original 1940s construction. Work continued apace to get it completed, just in time for the project to be cancelled in the next defence review.

The Ministry of Defence officially closed the airbase in 1959. Norfolk Gliding club was founded at the airfield in February that year and continues to operate from the site to this day.

Over the years, some of the veterans returned both to Tibenham and to Germany, where Walter Hassenpflug reunited with Frank Bertram who he had found by the stream all those years earlier. Memorials were constructed to the 445th on the airfield at Tibenham and, in 1990, to those on both sides lost in the battle at the crash site of Lt Chilton's lead ship at Ludwigsau, south of Kassel. Old enemies came together as friends, to swop experiences and remember the events that took so many lives.

Reconciliation

Memorial ceremony on the spot where Captain John Chilton crashed seventy-five years ago. (Author's collection)

Walter Hassenpflug became the German mission historian and a great deal of the information available both on the Internet and in books – including this one – is due to his painstaking research. He invested endless hours writing letters and reviewing documents and reports until he passed away in 2017.

Time marches on and the number of those actually there at the time has dwindled to a handful. But a new generation continues to visit the airfield, memorials and museums to keep the memories alive and see where their father, uncle, grandfather flew, fought and, in some cases, died.

Tibenham control tower just before it was demolished in 1975. (Norfolk Gliding Club archive)

Site 6 Quonset hut, 1944.

Site 6 Quonset hut, 2018.

Tibenham airfield in more peaceful times, now home to Norfolk Gliding club.

Appendices

Aircrew in alphabetical order

Rank	Last Name	First Name		Position	Crew	SQ	Serial #	Plane Nickname	Fate
S/St	Aaron	William		Radio Operator	Bolin	703	42-51355		KIA
2nd Lt	Abraham	Daniel	A	Navigator	Bruce	700	42-95128	Bonnie Vee	KIA
2nd Lt	Ajello	Louis	P	Navigator	Bolin	703	42-51355		KIA
2nd Lt	Alien	Harold	P	Co-pilot	Jones	702	41-29542	Rough House Kate	KIA
2nd Lt	Appleton	Daniel	H	Bombardier	Bruce	700	42-95128	Bonnie Vee	KIA
2nd Lt	Armstrong	Truman	Jr	Bombardier	Bolin	703	42-51355		KIA
T/Sgt	Ault	Robert	M	Engineer Top Turret Gunner	Miner	702	42-50961		POW
2nd Lt	Austin	George	R	Navigator-Bombardier	Carrow	700	42-110022	Patches	KIA
Sgt	Bagley	Robert	R	Waist Gunner	Golden	701	42-94863	Ole Baldy	PoW
S/Sgt	Bailey	Kyle	C	Top Turret Gunner	Isom	703	42-5081 1	Patty Girl	Returned
2nd Lt	Bailey	Herbert	E	Navigator	Dewey	701	42-50855		Manston
S/Sgt	Baldwin	Alan	M	Waist Gunner	Johnson	703	42-51342	Fridget Briget	PoW

139

Rank	Last Name	First Name		Position	Crew	SQ	Serial #	Plane Nickname	Fate
2nd Lt	Barben	Laurence	G	Co-pilot	Bolin	703	42-51355		KIA
T/Sgt	Barnes	Edward		Engineer	Isom	703	42-50811	Patty Girl	Returned
S/Sgt	Barnish	Francis	RE	Nose Turret Gunner	Warman	702	42-100308	Our Gal	POW
Sgt	Bartkow	Walter	J	Waist Gunner	Dewey	701	42-50855		Manston
2nd Lt	Bateman	Herbert	M	Navigator	Johnson	703	42-51342	Fridget Briget	KIA
1st Lt	Baynham	James	C	Pilot	Baynham	702	42-50383	King Kong	POW
2nd Lt	Bean	Corman	H	Navigator	Schaen	702	44-10511		POW
2nd Lt	Becker	John	J	Bombardier	Walther	701	44-10490	Big Jane	KIA
2nd Lt	Belitsos	Peter	S	Co-pilot	Bruland	701	41-28922	Texas Rose	POW
T/Sgt	Belouski	Roy	A	Radio Operator	Carrow	700	42-110022	Patches	KIA
S/Sgt	Bence	Raymond	E. Jr	Nose Turret Gunner	Fromm	703	42-51080		POW
T/Sgt	Bennet	Robert		Radio Operator	Mercer	703	42-51549		Manston
T/Sgt	Bergquist	Glenn	RA	Radio Operator	Walther	701	44-10490	Big Jane	KIA
1st Lt	Bertram	Francis	J	Navigator	Miner	702	42-50961		POW
Sgt	Biasetti	Ernest	J	Radio Operator	Potts	702	42-50340	Annie Mc Fannie	POW
2nd Lt	Bibb	Thomas	C	Navigator	Seeds	703	42-110073		KIA
S/Sgt	Bode	Ralph	H	Tail Gunner	Hansen	700	42-95078	Hare Force	KIA
2nd Lt	Boecher	Theodore	C	Bombardier	Golden	701	42-94863	Ole Baldy	POW
T/Sgt	Boldt	Howard	L	Engineer Top Turret Gunner	Baynham	702	42-50383	King Kong	POW

140

Rank	Surname	First	MI	Position	Pilot	Sqn	Serial	Aircraft	Fate
2nd Lt	Bolin	Roy	E	Pilot	Bolin	703	42-51355		KIA
T/Sgt	Boman	James	H	Radio Operator	Bruland	701	41-28922	Texas Rose	POW
2nd Lt	Boomhower	Edmund	F	Navigator	Golden	701	42-94863	Ole Baldy	POW
2nd Lt	Bousquet	Charles	M	Co-pilot	Baynham	702	42-50383	King Kong	POW
S/Sgt	Bowers	Lawrence	S	Waist Gunner	Miner	702	42-50961		POW
2nd Lt	Boykin	William	L	Co-pilot	Dewey	701	42-50855		Manston
2nd Lt	Brainard	Newell	W	Co-pilot	Carrow	700	42-110022	Patches	KIA
1st Lt	Brent	Donald	E	Pilot	Brent	702	42-50324	Eileen	KIA
S/Sgt	Bridgeo	James	L	Waist Gunner	Sollien	702	42-50321	Fort Worth Maid	KIA
2nd Lt	Bridges	Herbert	C. Jr	Co-pilot	Hansen	700	42-95078	Hare Force	POW
S/Sgt	Briggs	Merle	R	Waist Gunner	Chilton	703	42-51541		POW
Sgt	Broadway	Henry	Jr	Engineer Top Turret Gunner	Potts	702	42-50340	Annie Mc Fannie	KIA
2nd Lt	Brower	Ross	B	Navigator	Walther	701	44-10490	Big Jane	KIA
S/Sgt	Brower	William	N	Waist Gunner	Fromm	703	42-51080		POW
S/Sgt	Brown	Wilbur	E	Engineer Top Turret Gunner	Warman	702	42-100308	Our Gal	POW
2nd Lt	Bruce	William	S	Pilot	Bruce	700	42-95128	Bonnie Vee	POW
2nd Lt	Bruland	Palmer	M	Pilot	Bruland	701	41-28922	Texas Rose	POW
S/Sgt	Buch	John	E. Jr	Radio Operator	Seeds	703	42-110073		KIA
T/Sgt	Bugalecki	Donald	R	Engineer Top Turret Gunner	Krivik	702	42-100331	Percy	Old Buck

141

Rank	Last Name	First Name		Position	Crew	SQ	Serial #	Plane Nickname	Fate
S/Sgt	Byrd	Olen	C	Waist Gunner	Baynham	702	42-50383	King Kong	KIA
S/Sgt	Cabral	Santos	C	Waist Gunner	Uebelhoer	700	42-51547		Returned
T/Sgt	Cadden	John		Radio Operator	Krivik	702	42-100331	Percy	Old Buck
S/Sgt	Cannon	Robert	J	Waist Gunner	Hunter	700	42-94810	Terrible Terry's Terror	France
1st Lt	Capuano	Anthony		Nose Gunner	Smith	701	42-51710	710 E-Easy	Returned
2nd Lt	Carpenter	Wiliam	O	D/R Navigator	Smith	701	42-51710	710 E-Easy	Returned
1st Lt	Carrow	Raphael	E	Pilot	Carrow	700	42-110022	Patches	POW
Captain	Chilton	John	H	Pilot	Chilton	703	42-51541		KIA
1st Lt	Chima	Virgil		Co-pilot	Miner	702	42-50961		KIA
2nd Lt	Christie	Robert	C	Co-pilot	Golden	701	42-94863	Ole Baldy	POW
1st Lt	Cochran	Robert	D	Co-pilot	French	700	42-50784	Asbestos Alice	France
S/Sgt	Coffin	Lee	H	Tail Gunner	Fromm	703	42-51080		POW
2nd Lt	Collar	George	M	Bombardier	Schaen	702	44-10511		POW
T/Sgt	Collins	Robert	L	Radio Operator	Schaen	702	44-10511		POW
S/Sgt	Corman	James	E	Waist Gunner	French	700	42-50784		France
2nd Lt	Costley	Francis	W	Navigator	Warman	702	42-100308	Our Gal	KIA
Sgt	Cowart	Curtis	V	Waist Gunner	Smith	701	42-51710	710 E-Easy	Returned
2nd Lt	Cowgill	John	W	Navigator	Baynham	702	42-50383	King Kong	KIA
S/Sgt	Craig	Charles	O	Engineer Top Turret Gunner	Dewey	701	42-50855		Manston

Rank	Last Name	First Name	Initial	Position	Crew	No.	Serial	Aircraft	Status
Sgt	Crowley	James	J	Waist Gunner	Seeds	703	42-110073		KIA
2nd Lt	Cuddy	Norman	J	Navigator	Bruland	701	41-28922	Texas Rose	POW
F/O	Dale	Daniel		Navigator	Krivik	702	42-100331	Percy	KIA
Sgt	Danner	Maynard	R	Waist Gunner	Reynolds	701	42-50579	Little Audrey	POW
S/Sgt	Davis	Lonnie	O	Engineer Top Turret Gunner	Smith	701	42-51710	710 E-Easy	Returned
S/Sgt	Deckert	Charles	J. Jr	Waist Gunner	Elder	703	41-29579		POW
S/Sgt	Dengler	Nicholas	H	Waist Gunner	Carrow	700	42-110022	Patches	POW
2nd Lt	Dent	John	D	Pilotage Navigator	Sollien	702	42-50321	Fort Worth Maid	KIA
S/Sgt	Deshazer	Marvin		Nose Gunner	Swofford	701	42-51105	Sweetest Rose of Texas	Returned
T/Sgt	Devries	Paul	E	Engineer Top Turret Gunner	Elder	703	41-29579	Clay Pidgeon	POW
2nd Lt	Dewey	William	R	Pilot	Dewey	701	42-50855		Manston
S/Sgt	Dickerson	Paul		Waist Gunner	Isom	703	42-50811	Patty Girl	Returned
2nd Lt	Dimick	Nelson	L	Co-pilot	Pearson	700	44-10497		POW
F/O	Dobek	Henry	W	Navigator	Swofford	701	42-51105	Sweetest Rose of Texas	Returned
T/Sgt	Donahue	John	J	Radio Operator	Elder	703	41-29579	Clay Pidgeon	KIA
1st Lt	Donald	Myron	H	Pilot	Donald	702	42-51287	Flossye	KIA
Sgt	Douglas	James	M	Engineer Top Turret Gunner	Seeds	703	42-110073		KIA

Rank	Last Name	First Name		Position	Crew	SQ	Serial #	Plane Nickname	Fate
S/Sgt	Dove	Charles	M	Tail Gunner	Bruland	701	41-28922	Texas Rose	POW
1st Lt	Dowling	James	E	Bombardier	Johnson	703	42-51342	Fridget Bridget	POW
2nd Lt	Drake	Edward	J	Bombardier	Heitz	700	42-95210	Bugs Bunny	Belgium
S/Sgt	Durr	John	L	Waist Gunner	Elder	703	41-29579	Clay Pidgeon	POW
S/Sgt	Dykes	Willard	R	Waist Gunner	Swofford	701	42-51105	Sweetest Rose of Texas	Returned
T/Sgt	Eisenman	Arthur	P	Engineer Top Turret Gunner	Johnson	703	42-51342	Fridget Brigit	POW
1st Lt	Elder	Oliver	B	Pilot	Elder	703	41-29579	Clay Pidgeon	KIA
2nd Lt	Ellender	Roy	E	Co-pilot	Elder	703	41-29579	Clay Pidgeon	POW
S/Sgt	Ellson	John	E	Radio Operator	Dewey	701	42-50855		Manston
S/Sgt	Engleman	James	T	Engineer Top Turret Gunner	Reynolds	701	42-50579	Little Audrey	POW
T/Sgt	Eppley	George	S	Engineer Top Turret Gunner	Schaen	702	44-10511		POW
S/Sgt	Erickson	Jack	M	Radio Operator	Golden	701	42-94863	Ole Baldy	POW
2nd Lt	Fandler	Milton		Navigator	Mercer	703	42-51549		Manston
Sgt	Feltus	Edward	H	Waist Gunner	Golden	701	42-94863	Ole Baldy	POW
2nd Lt	Ferryman	L	D	Co-pilot	Hunter	700	42-94810	Terrible Terry's Terror	France
T/Sgt	Fields	James	T	Radio Operator	Baynham	702	42-50383	King Kong	KIA

144

T/Sgt	Fiske	Fred	N	Radio Operator	French	700	42-50784	Asbestos Alice	France
Sgt	Flach	Ferdinand	K	Nose Turret Gunner	Bruland	701	41-28922	Texas Rose	KIA
S/Sgt	Fleming	William	J	Waist Gunner	Bruce	700	42-95128	Bonnie Vee	KIA
2nd Lt	Flickner	William	E	Navigator / Nose Turret Gunner	Johnson	703	42-51342	Fridget Bridget	KIA
2nd Lt	Fluer	James	P	Radar Navigator	Uebelhoer	700	42-51547		Returned
S/Sgt	Forster	Carl	W	Waist Gunner	Warman	702	42-100308	Our Gal	KIA
T/Sgt	Fratta	Andrew		Engineer Top Turret Gunner	Jones	702	41-29542	Rough House Kate	KIA
Sgt	Frederiksen	Tage	R	Waist Gunner	Bolin	703	42-51355		KIA
1st Lt	French	John	E	Pilot	French	700	42-50784		France
2nd Lt	Freybler	James	R	Bombardier	Potts	702	42-50340	Annie Mc Fannie	KIA
1st Lt	Fromm	Richard	A	Pilot	Fromm	703	42-51080		POW
2nd Lt	Fulton	Robert		Navigator	Jones	702	41-29542	Rough House Kate	POW
T/Sgt	Galuszewski	Constantine		Engineer Top Turret Gunner	Brent	702	42-50324	Eileen	POW
S/Sgt	Galyon	Dwight	F	Tail Gunner	Pearson	700	44-10497		POW
2nd Lt	Geiszler	Martin	Jr	Co-pilot	Walther	701	44-10490	Big Jane	KIA
2nd Lt	George	Walter	E	Co-pilot	Brent	702	42-50324	Eileen	POW
T/Sgt	Giesler	Harold	W	Radio Operator	Hautman	703	42-109789	Mairzy Doats	POW
S/Sgt	Gilfoil	Joseph	H	Radio Operator	Miner	702	42-50961		KIA
2nd Lt	Globis	Edward	A	Co-pilot	Fromm	703	42-51080		KIA

145

THE KASSEL RAID, 27 SEPTEMBER 1944

Rank	Last Name	First Name		Position	Crew	SQ	Serial #	Plane Nickname	Fate
2nd Lt	Golden	William	F	Pilot	Golden	701	42-94863	Ole Baldy	KIA
T/Sgt	Graham	Charles	J	Radio Operator	Sollien	702	42-50321	Fort Worth Maid	POW
Captain	Graham	James		Deputy Group Commander	Uebelhoer	700	42-51547		Returned
S/Sgt	Gray	Stephen	J	Engineer Top Turret Gunner	Bruland	701	41-28922	Texas Rose	POW
Sgt	Gray	Eldon	E	Tail Gunner	Smith	701	42-51710	710 E-Easy	Returned
S/Sgt	Greenly	David	A	Nose Gunner	French	700	42-50784	Asbestos Alice	France
T/Sgt	Groves	Earl	B	Radio Operator	Mowat	703	42-51532	Hot Rock	KIA
2nd Lt	Hansen	Robert	N	Pilot	Hansen	700	42-95078		KIA
T/Sgt	Harrison	Homer	P	Engineer Top Turret Gunner	Heitz	700	42-95210	Bugs Bunny	Belgium
1st Lt	Hart	Billy	B	Co-pilot	Uebelhoer	700	42-51547		Returned
1st Lt	Hautman	Edward	F	Pilot	Hautman	703	42-109789	Mairzy Doats	KIA
1st Lt	Heisel	Jay		Navigator	Isom	703	42-50811	Patty Girl	Returned
1st Lt	Heitz	Raymond	V	Pilot	Heitz	700	42-95210	Bugs Bunny	Belgium
2nd Lt	Henard	Branch	H. Jr	Radar Navigator	Miner	702	42-50961		POW
F/O	Henrikson	Henry	J	Bombardier	Pearson	700	44-10497		KIA
T/Sgt	Hess	Calvin	F	Engineer Top Turret Gunner	Bruce	700	42-95128	Bonnie Vee	KIA

APPENDICES

									Manston
S/Sgt	Hoiten	Ted	E	Nose Gunner	Mercer	703	42-51549		
S/Sgt	Hollis	Norman	A	Waist Gunner	Walther	701	44-10490	Big Jane	KIA
S/Sgt	Hornsby	Elwyn	J	Waist Gunner	Hansen	700	42-95078	Hare Force	POW
T/Sgt	Howe	Orvel	G	Waist Gunner	Hautman	703	42-109789	Mairzy Doats	POW
S/Sgt	Howell	S	E. Jr	Waist Gunner	Hansen	700	42-95078	Hare Force	KIA
S/Sgt	Hubicz	John	S	Tail Gunner	Uebelhoer	700	42-51547		Returned
S/Sgt	Huddleston	Charles	A	Waist Gunner	French	700	42-50784	Asbestos Alice	France
2nd Lt	Hudelson	Wesley	L	Navigator	Sollien	702	42-50321	Fort Worth Maid	POW
2nd Lt	Hudson	Carlton	V	Pilotage Navigator	Chilton	703	42-51541		POW
S/Sgt	Huffman	Lee	RJ	Waist Gunner	Bruland	701	41-28922	Texas Rose	KIA
1st Lt	Hunter	William	F	Pilot	Hunter	700	42-94810	Terrible Terry's Terror	France
S/Sgt	Hurt	Brian	J	Tail Gunner	Schaen	702	44-10511		KIA
S/Sgt	Imhoff	Robert	C	Waist Gunner	Sollien	702	42-50321	Fort Worth Maid	KIA
1st Lt	Ische	Raymond	E	D/R Navigator	Chilton	703	42-51541		KIA
1st Lt	Isom	Cecil		Pilot	Isom	703	42-50811	Patty Girl	Returned
2nd Lt	Jackson	Charles	W	Pilotage Navigator	Miner	702	42-50961		POW
S/Sgt	Jackson	Floyd	L	Tail Gunner	Johnson	703	42-51342	Fridget Bridget	POW
T/Sgt	Jacobs	William	L	Engineer Top Turret Gunner	French	700	42-50784	Asbestos Alice	France
T/Sgt	Johnson	Robert	D	Engineer Top Turret Gunner	Pearson	700	44-10497		KIA
S/Sgt	Johnson	Edward	J	Waist Gunner	Schaen	702	44-10511		KIA

Rank	Last Name	First Name		Position	Crew	SQ	Serial #	Plane Nickname	Fate
Sgt	Johnson	Olin	D	Waist Gunner	Potts	702	42-50340	Annie Mc Fannie	KIA
1st Lt	Johnson	Joseph	E	Pilot	Johnson	703	42-51342	Fridget Bridget	POW
2nd Lt	Johnson	Cloys	V	Radar Navigator	Chilton	703	42-51541		POW
Sgt	Johnson	George		Waist Gunner	Dewey	701	42-50855		Manston
2nd Lt	Johnston	Robert	C	Co-pilot	Warman	702	42-100308	Our Gal	KIA
2nd Lt	Jones	Howard	A	Pilot	Jones	702	41-29542	Rough House Kate	POW
2nd Lt	Jones	Maynard	L	Navigator	Hautman	703	42-109789	Mairzy Doats	POW
1st Lt	Justus	Lonnie		Co-pilot	Isom	703	42-50811	Patty Girl	Returned
2nd Lt	Kathol	Gerald	J	Co-pilot	Potts	702	42-50340	Annie Mc Fannie	POW
2nd Lt	Keams	R	H	Navigator	Hunter	700	42-94810	Terrible Terry's Terror	France
2nd Lt	Kelly	Edward	M	Co-pilot	Johnson	703	42-51342	Fridget Bridget	POW
T/Sgt	Kielar	Anthony		Engineer Top Turret Gunner	Donald	702	42-51287	Flossye	KIA
S/Sgt	Kitchens	Alvis	O	Tail Gunner	Miner	702	42-50961		POW
S/Sgt	Klinefelter	William	R	Radio Operator	Smith	701	42-51710	710 E-Easy	Returned
S/Sgt	Knox	John	W	Tail Gunner	Baynham	702	42-50383	King Kong	POW
2nd Lt	Koenig	William	H	Co-pilot	Sollien	702	42-50321	Fort Worth Maid	KIA
T/Sgt	Kribs	Kenneth	W	Engineer Top Turret Gunner	Mercer	703	42-51549		Manston

1st Lt	Krivik	Stanley	E	Pilot	Krivik	702	42-100331	Percy	
1st Lt	Kugel	Arthur		Bombardier	Uebelhoer	700	42-51547		Returned
S/Sgt	Lamberson	Arthur	W	Waist Gunner	Miner	702	42-50961		POW
T/Sgt	Land	Thomas	W	Engineer Top Turret Gunner	Hautman	703	42-109789	Mairzy Doats	POW
Sgt	Larsen	Lars	E	Waist Gunner	Reynolds	701	42-50579	Little Audrey	KIA
S/Sgt	Larsen	Donald	W	Waist Gunner	Brent	702	42-50324	Eileen	KIA
Sgt	Laswell	Jack		Waist Gunner	Smith	701	42-51710	710 E-Easy	Returned
2nd Lt	Leary	John	F	Navigator	Heitz	700	42-95210	Buggs Bunny	Belgium
S/Sgt	Ledin	Herbert	A	Tail Gunner	Carrow	700	42-110022	Patches	POW
S/Sgt	Lee	Milton	H	Nose Turret Gunner	Jones	702	41-29542	Rough House Kate	POW
S/Sgt	Lello	Sylvester	V	Nose Turret Gunner	Mowat	703	42-51532	Hot Rock	KIA
S/Sgt	Lemons	John	R. Jr	Waist Gunner	Baynham	702	42-50383	King Kong	POW
T/Sgt	Lene	Russell	C	Engineer Top Turret Gunner	Fromm	703	42-51080		POW
2nd Lt	Lerch	Adolph	F	Co-pilot	Smith	701	42-51710	710 E-Easy	Returned
S/Sgt	Lied	Harry	J	Tail Gunner	Mercer	703	42-51549		Manston
S/Sgt	Linkletter	George	B	Nose Turret Gunner	Brent	702	42-50324	Eileen	KIA
S/Sgt	Loether	Charles	W	Waist Gunner	Carrow	700	42-110022	Patches	POW
Sgt	Long	Robert	M	Nose Turret Gunner	Reynolds	701	42-50579	Little Audrey	KIA
S/Sgt	Loving	John	M	Waist Gunner	Pearson	700	44-10497		POW
2nd Lt	Luongo	Michael	J	Co-pilot	Seeds	703	42-110073		KIA
1st Lt	MacGregor	Malcolm	J	Bombardier	Sollien	702	42-50321	Fort Worth Maid	POW

149

Rank	Last Name	First Name		Position	Crew	SQ	Serial #	Plane Nickname	Fate
T/Sgt	Mack	Fabian	S	Radio Operator	Heitz	700	42-95210	Bugs Bunny	KIA
S/Sgt	Mann	Milo	R	Tail Gunner	Walther	701	44-10490	Big Jane	KIA
S/Sgt	Maupin	Dale	C	Nose Turret Gunner	Hautman	703	42-109789	Mairzy Doats	POW
1st Lt	McCann	Charles	B	Navigator-Bombardier	Fromm	703	42-51080		POW
S/Sgt	McCormick	Glen	S	Ball Turret Gunner	Chilton	703	42-51541		POW
Major	McCoy	Don	W	Wing Commander	Chilton	703	42-51541		KIA
S/Sgt	McEntee	James	L	Waist Gunner	Donald	702	42-51287	Flossye	KIA
2nd Lt	McGough	Bobby	C	Co-pilot	Schaen	702	44-10511		POW
Sgt	Medlock	Leslie		Nose Gunner	Dewey	701	42-50855		Manston
2nd Lt	Meeks	Kenneth	L	Navigator / Nose Turret Gnr	Walther	701	44-10490	Big Jane	KIA
S/Sgt	Meier	Willis	A	Waist Gunner	Jones	702	41-29542	Rough House Kate	POW
1st Lt	Mercer	Jackson	C	Pilot	Mercer	703	42-51549		Manston
2nd Lt	Mercier	Harold	H	Bombardier	Brent	702	42-50324	Eileen	KIA
S/Sgt	Mesrobian	Haig		Waist Gunner	Uebelhoer	700	42-51547		Returned
S/Sgt	Miller	Ammi	H	Tail Gunner	Sollien	702	42-50321	Fort Worth Maid	POW
S/Sgt	Mills	Donald	W	Tail Gunner	Chilton	703	42-51541		POW
1st Lt	Miner	Reginald	R	Pilot	Miner	702	42-50961		POW

150

Rank	Last Name	First Name	Initial	Position	Name	Sqdn	Serial	Aircraft	Fate
Sgt	Mischel	Sigmund		Waist Gunner	Seeds	703	42-110073		KIA
S/Sgt	Modlin	Lawrence	A	Tail Gunner	Donald	702	42-51287	Flossye	KIA
Sgt	Montanez	Reuben	A	Tail Gunner	Dewey	701	42-50855		Manston
S/Sgt	Monzinqo	Jake	S	Radio Operator	Hunter	700	42-94810	Terrible Terry's Terror	France
S/Sgt	Morse	Stanley	H	Tail Gunner	Elder	703	41-29579	Clay Pidgeon	KIA
1st Lt	Mowat	William	J	Pilot	Mowat	703	42-51532	Hot Rock	KIA
T/Sgt	Myers	Theodore	J	Engineer Top Turret Gunner	Mowat	703	42-51532	Hot Rock	POW
S/Sgt	Neher	John	B. Jr	Waist Gunner	Mowat	703	42-51532	Hot Rock	KIA
2nd Lt	Nooriqian	George		Bombardier	Mercer	703	42-51549		Manston
S/Sgt	Ochevsky	Louis		Waist Gunner	Heitz	700	42-95210	Bugs Bunny	Belgium
T/Sgt	O'Keefe	Doyle	L	Radio Operator	Pearson	700	44-10497		POW
Sgt	Oleson	Robert	W	Waist Gunner	Bolin	703	42-51355		KIA
1st Lt	Omick	John	V	Bombardier	Miner	702	42-50961		POW
S/Sgt	Pakestein	Charles	G	Waist Gunner	Warman	702	42-100308	Our Gal	KIA
S/Sgt	Palm	Elroy	W	Waist Gunner	Heitz	700	42-95210	Bugs Bunny	Belgium
T/Sgt	Palmer	Charles	C. Jr	Engineer Top Turret Gunner	Hansen	700	42-95078		KIA
S/Sgt	Panconi	Victor	J	Nose Turret Gunner	Carrow	700	42-110022	Patches	KIA
S/Sgt	Parsons	Richard	L	Waist Gunner	Schaen	702	44-10511		KIA
S/Sgt	Paul	James	R	Waist Gunner	Krivik	702	42-100331	Percy	Old Buck
S/Sgt	Paulus	Raymond	J	Tail Gunner	Jones	702	41-29542	Rough House Kate	KIA
S/Sgt	Paulus	Fred	A	Waist Gunner	Bruce	700	42-95128	Bonnie Vee	KIA

Rank	Last Name	First Name		Position	Crew	SQ	Serial #	Plane Nickname	Fate
1st Lt	Pearson	Ralph	H	Pilot	Pearson	700	44-10497		POW
S/Sgt	Pendleton	Warren	B	Waist Gunner	Jones	702	41-29542	Rough House Kate	POW
S/Sgt	Phillips	Raymond		Tail Gunner	Isom	703	42-50811	Patty Girl	Returned
2nd Lt	Pile	Porter	M	Navigator	Hansen	700	42-95078	Hare Force	KIA
S/Sgt	Pimpinelli	Timothy		Waist Gunner	Swofford	701	42-51105	Sweetest Rose of Texas	Returned
S/Sgt	Plesa	Frank	T	Tail Gunner	Mowat	703	42-51532	Hot Rock	POW
T/Sgt	Pogovich	Peter		Radio Operator	Bruce	700	42-95128	Bonnie Vee	POW
2nd Lt	Potts	Herbert		Pilot	Potts	702	42-50340	Annie Mc Fannie	KIA
2nd Lt	Pouliot	Leo	P	Co-pilot	Mercer	703	42-51549		Manston
S/Sgt	Puto	Henry	A	Tail Gunner	Krivik	702	42-100331	Percy	Old Buck
T/Sgt	Rackis	Joseph	J	Radio Operator	Fromm	703	42-51080		POW
S/Sgt	Rand	William		Waist Gunner	Krivik	702	42-100331	Percy	Old Buck
S/Sgt	Ratchford	Robert	H	Engineer	Hunter	700	42-94810	Terrible Terry's Terror	France
S/Sgt	Ray	Raymond	W	Tail Gunner	Warman	702	42-100308	Our Gal	POW
T/Sgt	Reilly	Charles	H	Radio Operator	Johnson	703	42-51342	Fridget Bridget	POW
T/Sgt	Reinman	John	J	Radio Operator	Isom	703	42-50811	Patty Girl	Returned
2nd Lt	Reynolds	Donald	N	Pilot	Reynolds	701	42-50579	Little Audrey	POW

Rank	Last	First	MI	Position	Pilot/Co-pilot	Sq	Serial	Aircraft	Fate
2nd Lt	Robinson	Herbert	T	Co-pilot	Reynolds	701	42-50579	Little Audrey	POW
T/Sgt	Romine	Earl	C	Engineer Top Turret Gunner	Golden	701	42-94863	Ole Baldy	POW
Sgt	Sarber	Robert	W	Top Turret Gunner	Hunter	700	42-94810	Terrible Terry's Terror	France
2nd Lt	Scala	Hektor	V	Bombardier	Baynham	702	42-50383	King Kong	KIA
1st Lt	Schaen	James	W	Pilot	Schaen	702	44-10511		KIA
S/Sgt	Schaffer	Fred	C	Tail Gunner	Hunter	700	42-94810	Terrible Terry's Terror	France
2nd Lt	Scheu	M		Pilotage Navigator	Uebelhoer	700	42-51547		Returned
Sgt	Schooley	Orland	J	Tail Gunner	Bolin	703	42-51355		POW
S/Sgt	Schwartz	Herbert	R	Tail Gunner	French	700	42-50784	Asbestos Alice	France
Sgt	Scott	Roger	L	Waist Gunner	Potts	702	42-50340	Annie Mc Fannie	POW
2nd Lt	Seeds	Andrew	G	Pilot	Seeds	703	42-110073		KIA
Sgt	Selser	Joseph	A	Waist Gunner	Hunter	700	42-94810	Terrible Terry's Terror	France
S/Sgt	Selway	Donald		Waist Gunner	Mercer	703	42-51549		Manston
S/Sgt	Shaffer	Glenn	H	Tail Gunner	Bruce	700	42-95128	Bonnie Vee	KIA
S/Sgt	Shay	Robert	E	Waist Gunner	Chilton	703	42-51541		KIA
1st Lt	Shay	Arthur		Navigator	Isom	703	42-50811	Patty Girl	Returned
S/Sgt	Sheehan	Robert	C	Radio Operator	Reynolds	701	42-50579	Little Audrey	POW
S/Sgt	Shinske	John	C	Spare Gunner	Uebelhoer	700	42-51547		Returned
Sgt	Silverman	Rogers		Tail Gunner	Potts	702	42-50340	Annie Mc Fannie	POW

Rank	Last Name	First Name		Position	Crew	SQ	Serial #	Plane Nickname	Fate
T/Sgt	Sims	Robert	L	Radio Operator	Uebelhoer	700	42-51547		Returned
2nd Lt	Sirl	Joseph	F	Bombardier	Seeds	703	42-110073		KIA
S/Sgt	Sisco	Rubin	J	Waist Gunner	Johnson	703	42-51342	Fridget Bridget	POW
T/Sgt	Skomro	Joseph		Engineer Top Turret Gunner	Uebelhoer	700	42-51547		Returned
T/Sgt	Sloane	William	J	Radio Operator	Chilton	703	42-51541		POW
2nd Lt	Smets	Orville	P	Co-pilot	Mowat	703	42-51532	Hot Rock	KIA
S/Sgt	Smisek	Milton	C	Waist Gunner	Brent	702	42-50324	Eileen	KIA
2nd Lt	Smith	Frank	C	Co-pilot	Donald	702	42-51287	Flossye	POW
2nd Lt	Smith	Eric	W. Jr	Navigator	Donald	702	42-51287	Flossye	POW
S/Sgt	Smith	Douglas	P	Radio Operator	Warman	702	42-100308	Our Gal	KIA
1st Lt	Smith	Donald	H	Pilot	Smith	701	42-51710	710 E-Easy	Returned
2nd Lt	Smith	George	E	Bombardier	Hunter	700	42-94810	Terrible Terry's Terror	France
1st Lt	Smith	Ward	A	Co-pilot	Swofford	701	42-51105	Sweetest Rose of Texas	Returned
1st Lt	Smith	Clarence	H. Jr	Bombardier	Smith	701	42-51710	710 E-Easy	Returned
2nd Lt	Snidow	Carrol	G	Co-pilot	Hautman	703	42-109789	Mairzy Doats	POW

Rank	Surname	First	M	Position	Crew	Sqn	Serial	Aircraft	Fate
1st Lt	Sollien	Carl	J	Pilot	Sollien	702	42-50321	Fort Worth Maid	POW
S/Sgt	Spera	Thomas	G	Photographer-Observer	Hunter	700	42-94810	Terrible Terry's Terror	France
F/O	Spingler	John	L	Navigator / Bombardier	Mowat	703	42-51532	Hot Rock	KIA
1st Lt	Sprague	Wayne		Bombardier	Isom	703	42-50811	Patty Girl	Returned
2nd Lt	Stearns	Arthur	E	Navigator	Pearson	700	44-10497		KIA
T/Sgt	Stephens	William	C	Engineer Top Turret Gunner	Sollien	702	42-50321	Fort Worth Maid	KIA
Sgt	Stewart	Norman	J	Tail Gunner	Golden	701	42-94863	Ole Baldy	KIA
T/Sgt	Stidham	Jack	B	Radio Operator	Donald	702	42-51287	Flossye	POW
T/Sgt	Stremme	William	C	Radio Operator	Jones	702	41-29542	Rough House Kate	POW
S/Sgt	Stromberg	Clifford	N	Nose Gunner	Krivik	702	42-100331	Percy	Old Buck
T/Sgt	Sturdy	Howard	L	Engineer Top Turret Gunner	Chilton	703	42-51541		POW
S/Sgt	Sullivan	Hugh	J	Waist Gunner	Bruland	701	41-28922	Texas Rose	POW
2nd Lt	Sutherland	Harold	E	Co-pilot	Chilton	703	42-51541		KIA
1st Lt	Swofford	Paul		Pilot	Swofford	701	42-51105	Sweetest Rose of Texas	Returned
S/Sgt	Tachovsky	Harry	F	Waist Gunner	Pearson	700	44-10497		POW
S/Sgt	Tarbert	John	A	Waist Gunner	Hautman	703	42-109789	Mairzy Doats	KIA
S/Sgt	Thornton	Mertis 'Mac'	C Jr	Waist Gunner	Miner	702	42-50961		POW

THE KASSEL RAID, 27 SEPTEMBER 1944

Rank	Last Name	First Name		Position	Crew	SQ	Serial #	Plane Nickname	Fate
T/Sgt	Thum	Eugene	F	Radio Operator	Swofford	701	42-51105	Sweetest Rose of Texas	Returned
F/O	Tims	Robert	T	Navigator	French	700	42-50784	Asbestos Alice	France
T/Sgt	Tocket	Louis	T	Engineer Top Turret Gunner	Carrow	700	42-110022	Patches	KIA
1st Lt	Trefethen	Parker	S	Bombardier	Chilton	703	42-51541		POW
T/Sgt	Triplett	James	M	Radio Operator	Hansen	700	42-95078	Hare Force	KIA
2nd Lt	Trotta	Leonard	R	Co-pilot	Krivik	702	42-100331	Percy	Old Buck
Sgt	Twigg	Harry	G	Tail Gunner	Reynolds	701	42-50579		POW
Captain	Uebelhoer	Web	L	Pilot	Uebelhoer	700	42-51547		Returned
2nd Lt	Vedera	Harold	T	Co-pilot	Heitz	700	42-95210	Bugs Bunny	Belgium
2nd Lt	Vergos	Charles		Bombardier	Elder	703	41-29579	Clay Pidgeon	KIA
T/Sgt	Vernor	Richard	W	Engineer Top Turret Gunner	Walther	701	44-10490	Big Jane	KIA
T/Sgt	Vosburgh	Phillip		Engineer Top Turret Gunner	Swofford	701	42-51105	Sweetest Rose of Texas	Returned
S/Sgt	Wagner	W	E	Waist Gunner	Isom	703	42-50811	Patty Girl	Returned
S/Sgt	Waldron	Gordon	F	Tail Gunner	Hautman	703	42-109789	Mairzy Doats	KIA
S/Sgt	Waller	Joseph	V	Tail Gunner	Swofford	701	42-51105	Sweetest Rose of Texas	Returned
S/Sgt	Walston	Walter	J	Waist Gunner	Donald	702	42-51287	Flossye	KIA

Rank	Last Name	First Name	N	Role	Pilot	Sqdn	Serial	Aircraft	Status
1st Lt	Walther	Edgar	N	Pilot	Walther	701	44-10490	Big Jane	POW
2nd Lt	Warman	Leslie	E	Pilot	Warman	702	42-100308	Our Gal	KIA
S/Sgt	Watson	Maynard	B	Tail Gunner	Heitz	700	42-95210	Bugs Bunny	Belgium
S/Sgt	Watts	Woodard	C	Tail Gunner	Brent	702	42-50324	Eileen	KIA
Sgt	Weatherly	Charles	E	Engineer Top Turret Gunner	Bolin	703	42-51355		KIA
T/Sgt	Weiner	Sammy	S	Radio Operator	Brent	702	42-50324	Eileen	POW
1st Lt	Weinstein	Ira	P	Bombardier	Donald	702	42-51287	Flossye	POW
S/Sgt	Wheaton	Harry	L	Waist Gunner	Mercer	703	42-51549		Manston
Sgt	Wheeler	Clare	L	Tail Gunner	Seeds	703	42-110073		KIA
1st Lt	Whidden	Harold	P. Jr	Navigator	Elder	703	41-29579	Clay Pidgeon	POW
1st Lt	Whitefield	Donald		D/R Navigator	Uebelhoer	700	42-51547		Returned
1st Lt	Willet	John	P. Jr	Co-pilot	Bruce	700	42-95128	Bonnie Vee	KIA
S/Sgt	Williams	Joseph	F	Waist Gunner	Fromm	703	42-51080		POW
S/Sgt	Williams	Everette	L	Waist Gunner	Mowat	703	42-51532	Hot Rock	KIA
2nd Lt	Wilski	Joseph	A	Bombardier	Jones	702	41-29542	Rough House Kate	POW
S/Sgt	Wise	John	F	Waist Gunner	Walther	701	44-10490	Big Jane	KIA
1st Lt	Withey	James	T	Navigator-Bombardier	Reynolds	701	42-50579	Little Audrey	POW
2nd Lt	Woodley	John	C	Bombardier	Hansen	700	42-95078	Hare Force	POW
2nd Lt	Zornow	Dale	F	Navigator	Potts	702	42-50340	Annie Mc Fannie	KIA

KIA = Killed in action
KIA = Murdered

Aircraft by squadron

Serial no.	Name	Sqd. and reg	Crew	Fate
42-95078	HARE FORCE	700 C IS	HANSEN	SHOT DOWN GERMANY
42-50784	ABESTOS ALICE	700 D IS	FRENCH	C/L FRANCE
42-51547	BAD PENNY	700 E IS	UEBELHOER	RETURNED
42-110022	PATCHES	700 F IS	CARROW	SHOT DOWN GERMANY
42-9810	TERRIBLE TERRY'S TERROR	700 J+IS	HUNTER	C/L FRANCE
44-10497		700P IS	PEARSON	SHOT DOWN GERMANY
42-95210	BONNIE VEE	700R+IS	BRUCE	SHOT DOWN GERMANY
42-95210	BUGS BUNNY	700U IS	HEITZ	C/L BELGIUM
42-50855		701A MK	DEWEY	C/L MANSTON KENT
42-94921	TAHELENBAK	701B+MK	McCLELLAND	ABORTED
44-40294	SLOSSIE	701C MK	FROST	ABORTED
42-51710	710 E-Easy	701 E MK	SMITH	RETURNED
42-51105	SWEETEST ROSE OF TEXAS	701O MK	SWOFFORD	RETURNED
41-28922	TEXAS ROSE	701Q MK	BRULAND	SHOT DOWN GERMANY
42-50579	LITTLE AUDREY	701R+MK	REYNOLDS	SHOT DOWN GERMANY
42-94939	HEAVENLY BODY	701S MK	WILKINS	ABORTED
42-94863	OLE BALDY	701T MK	GOLDEN	SHOT DOWN GERMANY
44-10490	BIG JANE	701Z MK	WALTHER	SHOT DOWN GERMANY
41-29542	ROUGHHOUSE KATE	702A WV	JONES	SHOT DOWN GERMANY

42-50340	ANNIE MCFANNIE	702B WV	POTTS	SHOT DOWN GERMANY
44-10511		702C WV	SCHAEN	SHOT DOWN GERMANY
42-110073	STEADY HEADY	702O WV	SEEDS	SHOT DOWN GERMANY
42-100308	OUR GAL	702Q WV	WARMAN	SHOT DOWN GERMANY
42-50324	EILEEN	702S WV	BRENT	SHOT DOWN GERMANY
42-100331	PERCY	702U WV	KRIVIK	CRASHED OLD BUCKENHAM
42-50321	FORT WORTH MAID	702V WV	SOLLIEN	SHOT DOWN GERMANY
42-50961		702W WV	MINER	SHOT DOWN GERMANY
42-50383	KING KONG	702X WV	BAYNHAM	SHOT DOWN GERMANY
42-51287	FLOSSYE	702Y WV	DONALD	SHOT DOWN GERMANY
42-109789	MAIRZY DOATS	703A RN	HAUTMAN	SHOT DOWN GERMANY
42-50811	PATTY GIRL	703E+RN	ISOM	RETURNED
42-51549		703G RN	MERCER	C/L MANSTON KENT
42-51541		703H RN	CHILTON	SHOT DOWN GERMANY
42-51342	FRIDGET BRIDGET	703I RN	JOHNSON	SHOT DOWN GERMANY
42-51355		703K RN	BOLIN	SHOT DOWN GERMANY
41-29579	CLAY PIDGEON	703N RN	ELDER	SHOT DOWN GERMANY
44-40250		703O RN	SCHNEIDER	ABORTED
42-51532	HOT ROCK	703P RN	MOWAT	SHOT DOWN GERMANY
42-51080		703U RN	FROMM	SHOT DOWN GERMANY

Missing aircrews fates

MACR				FO					
702	Dale	Daniel	J	2nd Lt	KIA	T125565	Navigator	N/A	42-100331
701	Bruland	Palmer	M	2nd Lt	POW	O-763480	Pilot	9386	41-28922
701	Belitsos	Peter	S	2nd Lt	POW	O-822625	Co-pilot	9386	41-28922
701	Cuddy	Norman	J	2nd Lt	POW	O-747646	Navigator	9386	41-28922
701	Flach	Ferdinand	E	Sgt	KIA	37540396	Nose Turret Gunner	9386	41-28922
701	Gray	Stephen	J	S/Sgt	POW	11015475	Flight Engineer	9386	41-28922
701	Boman	James	E	T/Sgt	POW	39557815	Radio Operator	9386	41-28922
701	Huffman	Lee	R J	S/Sgt	KIA	34203002	Left Waist Gunner	9386	41-28922
701	Sullivan	Hugh	J	S/Sgt	POW	39115320	Right Waist Gunner	9386	41-28922
701	Dove	Charles	M	S/Sgt	POW	35226700	Tail Turret Gunner	9386	41-28922
702	Jones	Howard	A	2nd Lt	POW	O-699674	Pilot	9570	41-29542
702	Allen	Harold	P	2nd Lt	KIA	O-772248	Co-pilot	9570	41-29542
702	Fulton	Robert	J	2nd Lt	POW	O-716408	Navigator	9570	41-29542
702	Wilski	Joseph	A	2nd Lt	POW	O-716799	Bombardier	9570	41-29542
702	Fratta	Andrew	(nmi)	T/Sgt	KIA	12121322	Flight Engineer	9570	41-29542
702	Stremme	William	C	T/Sgt	POW	13112364	Radio Operator	9570	41-29542
702	Lee	Milton	(nmi)	S/Sgt	POW	39854610	Ball Turret Gunner	9570	41-29542
702	Paulus	Raymond	J	S/Sgt	KIA	37573772	Left Waist Gunner	9570	41-29542

Sqn	Last Name	First Name	Init	Rank	Status	Serial	Role	Aircraft	Serial No.
702	Pendleton	Warren	B	T/Sgt	POW	36692466	Right Waist Gunner	9570	41-29542
702	Meier	Willis	A	S/Sgt	POW	17121166	Tail Turret Gunner	9570	41-29542
703	Elder	Oliver	B	1st Lt	KIA	O-817826	Pilot	9387	41-29579
703	Ellender	Roy	E	2nd Lt	POW	O-1996104	Co-pilot	9387	41-29579
703	Whidden	Harold	P	1st Lt	POW	O-708301	Navigator	9387	41-29579
703	Vergos	Charles	(nmi)	2nd Lt	KIA	O-1996085	Bombardier	9387	41-29579
703	DeVries	Paul	E	T/Sgt	POW	31126075	Flight Engineer	9387	41-29579
703	Donahue	John	J	T/Sgt	KIA	33524628	Radio Operator	9387	41-29579
703	Deckert	Charles	J	S/Sgt	POW	32876559	Left Waist Gunner	9387	41-29579
703	Durr	John	L	S/Sgt	POW	35685514	Right Waist Gunner	9387	41-29579
703	Morse	Stanley	H	S/Sgt	KIA	32672315	Tail Turret Gunner	9387	41-29579
702	Sollien	Carl	J	1st Lt	POW	O-819197	Pilot	9911	42-50321
702	Koenig	William	H	2nd Lt	KIA	O-823880	Co-pilot	9911	42-50321
702	Hudelson	Wesley	L	2nd Lt	POW	O-711527	Navigator	9911	42-50321
702	Dent	John	D	2nd Lt	KIA	O-769013	Nose Turret Gunner	9911	42-50321
702	MacGregor	Malcolm	J	1st Lt	POW	O-898023	Bombardier	9911	42-50321
702	Stephens	William	C	T/Sgt	KIA	16084038	Flight Engineer	9911	42-50321
702	Graham	Charles	J	T/Sgt	POW	36481757	Radio Operator	9911	42-50321
702	Bridges	James	L	S/Sgt	KIA	31370167	Left Waist Gunner	9911	42-50321
702	Imhoff	Robert	C	S/Sgt	KIA	19199767	Right Waist Gunner	9911	42-50321
702	Miller	Ammi	H	S/Sgt	POW	39335728	Tail Turret Gunner	9911	42-50321

Squadron	Last Name	First Name	MI	Rank	Status	Serial	Position	No.	Aircraft
702	Brent	Donald	E	1st Lt	KIA	O-747730	Pilot	9388	42-50324
702	George	Walter	E	2nd Lt	POW	O-826917	Co-pilot	9388	42-50324
702	Linkletter	George	B	S/Sgt	KIA	33539866	Nose Turret Gunner	9388	42-50324
702	Mercier	Harold	M	2nd Lt	KIA	O-688502	Bombardier	9388	42-50324
702	Galuszewski	Constant	S	T/Sgt	POW	32583006	Flight Engineer	9388	42-50324
702	Weiner	Sammy	S	T/Sgt	POW	19061851	Radio Operator	9388	42-50324
702	Larson	Donald	W	S/Sgt	KIA	39571317	Left Waist Gunner	9388	42-50324
702	Smisek	Milton	C	S/Sgt	KIA	17937617	Right Waist Gunner	9388	42-50324
702	Watts	Woodard	C	S/Sgt	KIA	34366107	Tail Turret Gunner	9388	42-50324
702	Potts	Herbert	(nmi)	2nd Lt	KIA	O-702333	Pilot	9389	42-50340
702	Kathol	Gerald	J	2nd Lt	POW	O-719677	Co-pilot	9389	42-50340
702	Zornow	Dale	F	2nd Lt	KIA	O-722412	Navigator	9389	42-50340
702	Freybler	James	R	2nd Lt	KIA	O-716855	Bombardier	9389	42-50340
702	Broadway	Henry		Sgt	KIA	38420812	Flight Engineer	9389	42-50340
702	Biasetti	Ernest	J	Sgt	POW	12006731	Radio Operator	9389	42-50340
702	Scott	Roger	L	Sgt	POW	19149760	Left Waist Gunner	9389	42-50340
702	Johnson	Olin	D	Sgt	KIA	37682457	Right Waist Gunner	9389	42-50340
702	Silverman	Roger	(nmi)	Sgt	POW	32098141	Tail Turret Gunner	9389	42-50340
702	Baynham	James	C	1st Lt	POW	O-653834	Pilot	9390	42-50383
702	Bousquet	Charles	M	2nd Lt	POW	O-217621	Co-pilot	9390	42-50383
702	Cowgill	John	W	2nd Lt	KIA	O-703710	Navigator	9390	42-50383

Sqn	Last Name	First Name	MI	Rank	Status	Serial No.	Position	A/C No.	A/C Serial
702	Scala	Hector	V	2nd Lt	KIA	O-552862	Bombardier	9390	42-50383
702	Boldt	Howard	L	T/Sgt	POW	18188472	Flight Engineer	9390	42-50383
702	Fields	James	T	T/Sgt	KIA	19486421	Radio Operator	9390	42-50383
702	Lemons	John	Ray	S/Sgt	POW	38428817	Left Waist Gunner	9390	42-50383
702	Byrd	Olen	C	S/Sgt	KIA	38118508	Right Waist Gunner	9390	42-50383
702	Knox	John	W	S/Sgt	POW	35625348	Tail Turret Gunner	9390	42-50383
701	Reynolds	Donald	N	2nd Lt	POW	O-819611	Pilot	9761	42-50579
701	Robinson	Herbert	T	2nd Lt	POW	O-824230	Co-pilot	9761	42-50579
701	Withey	James	T	1st Lt	POW	O-712729	Navigator	9761	42-50579
701	Long	Robert	M	Sgt	KIA	33515646	Nose Turret Gunner	9761	42-50579
701	Engleman	James	T	S/Sgt	POW	12179349	Flight Engineer	9761	42-50579
701	Sheehan	Robert	C	S/Sgt	POW	34684527	Radio Operator	9761	42-50579
701	Larsen	Lars	E	Sgt	KIA	32778375	Left Waist Gunner	9761	42-50579
701	Dunner	Maynard	R	Sgt	POW	33500104	Right Waist Gunner	9761	42-50579
701	Twigg	Harry	G	Sgt	POW	33361137	Tail Turret Gunner	9761	42-50579
702	Miner	Reginald	R	1st Lt	POW	O-516540	Pilot	9571	42-50961
702	Chima	Virgil	(nmi)	1st Lt	KIA	O-704361	Co-pilot	9571	42-50961
702	Bertram	Francis	J	1st Lt	POW	O-713097	Navigator	9571	42-50961
702	Henard	Branch	H	2nd Lt	POW	O-703638	Radar Navigator	9571	42-50961
702	Jackson	Charles	W	2nd Lt	POW	O-715413	Nose Turret Gunner	9571	42-50961
702	Omick	John	V	1st Lt	POW	O-672968	Bombardier	9571	42-50961

Sqn	Last Name	First Name	MI	Rank	Status	Serial	Position	No.	Aircraft
702	Ault	Robert	M	T/Sgt	POW	18104421	Flight Engineer	9571	42-50961
702	Gilfoil	Joseph	H	S/Sgt	KIA	31270331	Radio Operator	9571	42-50961
702	Lamberson	Arthur	W	S/Sgt	POW	33604181	Ball Turret Gunner	9571	42-50961
702	Thornton	Mertis	C	S/Sgt	POW	34623735	Left Waist Gunner	9571	42-50961
702	Bowers	Lawrence	S	S/Sgt	POW	34765545	Right Waist Gunner	9571	42-50961
702	Kitchens	Alvis	O	S/Sgt	POW	38519361	Tail Turret Gunner	9571	42-50961
703	Fromm	Richard	A	1st Lt	POW	O-320988	Pilot	9762	42-51080
703	Globis	Edward	A	2nd Lt	KIA	O-326923	Co-pilot	9762	42-51080
703	McCann	Charles	B	1st Lt	POW	O-709955	Navigator	9762	42-51080
703	Bence	Raymond	E	S/Sgt	POW	11139308	Nose Turret Gunner	9762	42-51080
703	Lene	Russell	C	T/Sgt	POW	17114588	Flight Engineer	9762	42-51080
703	Rackis	Joseph	J	T/Sgt	POW	11095890	Radio Operator	9762	42-51080
703	Brower	William	N	S/Sgt	POW	42016172	Left Waist Gunner	9762	42-51080
703	Williams	Joseph	F	S/Sgt	POW	6152411	Right Waist Gunner	9762	42-51080
703	Coffin	Lee	H	S/Sgt	POW	31406316	Tail Turret Gunner	9762	42-51080
702	Donald	Myron	H	1st Lt	KIA	O-696339	Pilot	9391	42-51287
702	Smith	Frank	C	2nd Lt	POW	O-706005	Co-pilot	9391	42-51287
702	Smith	Eric	W	2nd Lt	POW	O-768906	Navigator	9391	42-51287
702	Weinstein	Ira	P	1st Lt	POW	O-694482	Bombardier	9391	42-51287
702	Kielar	Anthony	(nmi)	T/Sgt	KIA	12096135	Flight Engineer	9391	42-51287
702	Stidham	Jack	B	T/Sgt	POW	35790866	Radio Operator	9391	42-51287

Sqdn	Last Name	First Name	MI	Rank	Status	Serial No.	Position	No.	Tail No.
702	McEntee	James	L	S/Sgt	KIA	35056796	Left Waist Gunner	9391	42-51287
702	Walston	Walter	J	S/Sgt	KIA	18218241	Right Waist Gunner	9391	42-51287
702	Modlin	Lawrence	A	S/Sgt	KIA	37536367	Tail Turret Gunner	9391	42-51287
703	Johnson	Joseph	E	1st Lt	POW	O-817687	Pilot	9392	42-51342
703	Kelly	Edward	M	2nd Lt	POW	O-1291476	Co-pilot	9392	42-51342
703	Bateman	Herbert	M	2nd Lt	KIA	O-716591	Navigator	9392	42-51342
703	Dowling	James	E	FO	POW	T125608	Bombardier	9392	42-51342
703	Flickner	William	E	2nd Lt	KIA	O-768856	Nose Turret Gunner	9392	42-51342
703	Eisenman	Arthur	F	T/Sgt	POW	16009835	Flight Engineer	9392	42-51342
703	Reilly	Charles	H	T/Sgt	POW	12086559	Radio Operator	9392	42-51342
703	Sisco	Rubin	J	S/Sgt	POW	38370137	Left Waist Gunner	9392	42-51342
703	Baldwin	Alan	M	S/Sgt	POW	33673360	Right Waist Gunner	9392	42-51342
703	Jackson	Floyd	L	S/Sgt	POW	34818919	Tail Turret Gunner	9392	42-51342
703	Bolin	Roy	E	2nd Lt	KIA	O-705107	Pilot	9393	42-51355
703	Barben	Lawrence	G	2nd Lt	KIA	O-771270	Co-pilot	9393	42-51355
703	Ajello	Louis	P	2nd Lt	KIA	O-722971	Navigator	9393	42-51355
703	Armstrong	Truman	(nmi)	2nd Lt	KIA	O-773278	Bombardier	9393	42-51355
703	Weatherly	Charles	E	Sgt	KIA	38436326	Flight Engineer	9393	42-51355
703	Aaron	William	(nmi)	S/Sgt	KIA	11072501	Radio Operator	9393	42-51355
703	Frederickson	Tage	R	Sgt	KIA	32858310	Left Waist Gunner	9393	42-51355
703	Oleson	Robert	W	Sgt	KIA	39618538	Right Waist Gunner	9393	42-51355

703	Schooley	Orland	J	Sgt	POW	33642320	Tail Turret Gunner	9393	42-51355
703	Mowat	William	J	1st Lt	KIA	O-810229	Pilot	9572	42-51532
703	Smets	Orville	P	2nd Lt	KIA	O-713603	Co-pilot	9572	42-51532
703	Springler	John	L	F/O	KIA	T-125579	Navigator	9572	42-51532
703	Myers	Theodore	J	T/Sgt	POW	37722219	Flight Engineer	9572	42-51532
703	Groves	Earl	B	T/Sgt	KIA	32581359	Radio Operator	9572	42-51532
703	Lello	Sylvester	V	S/Sgt	KIA	31145800	Ball Turret Gunner	9572	42-51532
703	Williams	Everette	L	S/Sgt	KIA	14164570	Left Waist Gunner	9572	42-51532
703	Neher	John	B	S/Sgt	KIA	37722061	Right Waist Gunner	9572	42-51532
703	Plesa	Frank	T	S/Sgt	POW	37722733	Tail Turret Gunner	9572	42-51532
703	Chilton	John	H	Capt	KIA	0-811015	Pilot	9394	42-51541
703	McCoy	Don	W	Major	KIA	0-740232	Command Pilot	9394	42-51541
703	Sutherland	Harold	E	2nd Lt	KIA	0-817862	Co-pilot	9394	42-51541
703	Ische	Raymond	E	1st Lt	KIA	0-700886	Observer (RN/RB)	9394	42-51541
703	Johnson	Cloys	V	2nd Lt	POW	0-767928	Navigator	9394	42-51541
703	Hudson	Carlton	V	2nd Lt	POW	0-712142	Nose Turret Gunner	9394	42-51541
703	Trefethen	Parker	S	1st Lt	POW	0-696281	Bombardier	9394	42-51541
703	Sturdy	Howard	L	T/Sgt	POW	36569200	Flight Engineer	9394	42-51541
703	Sloane	William	J	T/Sgt	POW	16092605	Radio Operator	9394	42-51541
703	McCormick	Glen	S	S/Sgt	POW	6932898	Ball Turret Gunner	9394	42-51541

703	Shay	Robert	E	S/Sgt	POW	37467644	Left Waist Gunner	9394	42-51541
703	Briggs	Merle	R	S/Sgt	POW	31317202	Right Waist Gunner	9394	42-51541
703	Mills	Donald	W	S/Sgt	POW	15132305	Tail Turret Gunner	9394	42-51541
701	Golden	William	F	2nd Lt	KIA	O-807838	Pilot	9395	42-94863
701	Christie	Robert	C	2nd Lt	POW	O-824038	Co-pilot	9395	42-94863
701	Boomhower	Edmund	F	2nd Lt	POW	O-712780	Navigator	9395	42-94863
701	Boecher	Theodore	C	2nd Lt	POW	O-891372	Bombardier	9395	42-94863
701	Romine	Earl	C	T/Sgt	POW	35753053	Flight Engineer	9395	42-94863
701	Erickson	Jack	M	S/Sgt	POW	39410882	Radio Operator	9395	42-94863
701	Feltus	Edward	H	Sgt	POW	42008001	Left Waist Gunner	9395	42-94863
701	Bagley	Robert	R	Sgt	POW	17065934	Right Waist Gunner	9395	42-94863
701	Stewart	Norman	J	Sgt	KIA	16139151	Tail Turret Gunner	9395	42-94863
700	Hansen	Robert	N	2nd Lt	KIA	O-700609	Pilot	9396	42-95078
700	Bridges	Herbert	C	2nd Lt	POW	O-768429	Co-pilot	9396	42-95078
700	Pile	Porter	M	2nd Lt	KIA	O-719140	Navigator	9396	42-95078
700	Woodley	John	C	2nd Lt	POW	O-879436	Bombardier	9396	42-95078
700	Palmer	Charles	C	T/Sgt	KIA	19083921	Flight Engineer	9396	42-95078
700	Triplett	James	E	T/Sgt	KIA	39202130	Radio Operator	9396	42-95078
700	Hornsby	Elwyn	J	Sgt	POW	38487741	Left Waist Gunner	9396	42-95078
700	Howell	S	E	Sgt	KIA	38487753	Right Waist Gunner	9396	42-95078
700	Bode	Ralph	H	Sgt	KIA	16117549	Tail Turret Gunner	9396	42-95078

167

700	Bruce	William	S	2nd Lt	POW	O-518582	Pilot	9397	42-95128
700	Willett	John	P	1st Lt	KIA	O-432218	Co-pilot	9397	42-95128
700	Abraham	Danial	A	2nd Lt	KIA	O-717365	Navigator	9397	42-95128
700	Appleton	Daniel	H	2nd Lt	KIA	O-681770	Bombardier	9397	42-95128
700	Hess	Calvin	F	T/Sgt	KIA	35057106	Flight Engineer	9397	42-95128
700	Pogovich	Peter	(nmi)	T/Sgt	POW	32887620	Radio Operator	9397	42-95128
700	Fleming	William	J	S/Sgt	KIA	37527992	Left Waist Gunner	9397	42-95128
700	Paulus	Fred	A	S/Sgt	KIA	35758806	Right Waist Gunner	9397	42-95128
700	Shaffer	Glenn	H	S/Sgt	KIA	33764321	Tail Turret Gunner	9397	42-95128
702	Warman	Lesle	E	2nd Lt	KIA	O-817797	Pilot	9763	42-100308
702	Johnson	Robert	C	2nd Lt	KIA	O-826183	Co-pilot	9763	42-100308
702	Costley	Francis	W	2nd Lt	KIA	O-713001	Navigator	9763	42-100308
702	Barnish	Francis	R E	S/Sgt	POW	31415124	Nose Turret Gunner	9763	42-100308
702	Brown	Wilbur	E	S/Sgt	POW	33721118	Flight Engineer	9763	42-100308
702	Smith	Douglas	P	S/Sgt	KIA	39559850	Radio Operator	9763	42-100308
702	Ray	Raymond	W	S/Sgt	POW	35875778	Left Waist Gunner	9763	42-100308
702	Pakestein	Charles	G	S/Sgt	KIA	42000885	Right Waist Gunner	9763	42-100308
702	Forster	Carl	W	S/Sgt	KIA	33832889	Tail Turret Gunner	9763	42-100308
703	Hartman	Edward	F	1st Lt	KIA	O-697358	Pilot	9398	42-109789
703	Snidow	Carroll	G	2nd Lt	POW	O-821104	Co-pilot	9398	42-109789

703	Jones	Maynard	L	2nd Lt	POW	O-712837	Navigator	9398	42-109789
703	Maupin	Dale	C	S/Sgt	POW	37537180	Nose Turret Gunner	9398	42-109789
703	Land	Thomas	V	T/Sgt	POW	35795621	Flight Engineer	9398	42-109789
703	Giesler	Harold	W	T/Sgt	POW	37302826	Radio Operator	9398	42-109789
703	Tarbert	John	A	S/Sgt	KIA	6947526	Left Waist Gunner	9398	42-109789
703	Howe	Orvel	G	T/Sgt	POW	6570005	Right Waist Gunner	9398	42-109789
703	Waldron	Gordon	F	S/Sgt	KIA	36549147	Tail Turret Gunner	9398	42-109789
700	Carrow	Raphael	E	1st Lt	POW	O-812546	Pilot	9399	42-110022
700	Brainard	Newell	W	2nd Lt	KIA	O-812929	Co-pilot	9399	42-110022
700	Austin	George	R.	2nd Lt	KIA	O-716698	Navigator	9399	42-110022
700	Panconi	Victor	J	S/Sgt	KIA	39099421	Nose Turret Gunner	9399	42-110022
700	Tocket	Louis	T	T/Sgt	KIA	35215173	Flight Engineer	9399	42-110022
700	Belouski	Roy	A	T/Sgt	KIA	39440654	Radio Operator	9399	42-110022
700	Dengler	Nicholas	H	S/Sgt	POW	37662981	Left Waist Gunner	9399	42-110022
700	Loether	Charles	W	S/Sgt	POW	33420032	Right Waist Gunner	9399	42-110022
700	Ledin	Herbert	A	S/Sgt	POW	31351923	Tail Turret Gunner	9399	42-110022
703	Seeds	Andrew	G	2nd Lt	KIA	O-700553	Pilot	9400	42-110073
703	Luongo	Michael	J	2nd Lt	KIA	O-711225	Co-pilot	9400	42-110073
703	Bibb	Thomas	C	2nd Lt	KIA	O-2058401	Navigator	9400	42-110073
703	Sirl	Joseph	H	2nd Lt	KIA	O-773006	Bombardier	9400	42-110073
703	Douglas	James	E	Sgt	KIA	32887504	Flight Engineer	9400	42-110073

THE KASSEL RAID, 27 SEPTEMBER 1944

703	Buch	John	E	T/Sgt	KIA	13157636	Radio Operator	9400	42-110073
703	Mischel	Sigmund	C	Sgt	KIA	19162503	Left Waist Gunner	9400	42-110073
703	Crowley	James	J	Sgt	KIA	31241510	Right Waist Gunner	9400	42-110073
703	Wheeler	Clare	L	Sgt	KIA	36816304	Tail Turret Gunner	9400	42-110073
701	Walther	Edgar	N	1st Lt	POW	O-697381	Pilot	9383	44-10490
701	Geiszler	Martin		2nd Lt	KIA	O-758064	Co-pilot	9383	44-10490
701	Brower	Ross	B	2nd Lt	KIA	O-717330	Navigator	9383	44-10490
701	Becker	John	J	2nd Lt	KIA	O-768984	Bombardier	9383	44-10490
701	Meeks	Kenneth	L	2nd Lt	KIA	O-706890	Nose Turret Gunner	9383	44-10490
701	Vernor	Richard	W	T/Sgt	KIA	36479868	Flight Engineer	9383	44-10490
701	Bergquist	Glenn	R A	T/Sgt	KIA	18120232	Radio Operator	9383	44-10490
701	Wise	John	F	S/Sgt	KIA	39465098	Left Waist Gunner	9383	44-10490
701	Hollis	Norman	A	S/Sgt	KIA	39562159	Right Waist Gunner	9383	44-10490
701	Mann	Milo	R	S/Sgt	KIA	36391267	Tail Turret Gunner	9383	44-10490
700	Pearson	Ralph	H	1st Lt	POW	O-817738	Pilot	9384	44-10497
700	Dimick	Nelson	L	2nd Lt	POW	O-822396	Co-pilot	9384	44-10497
700	Stearns	Arthur	E	2nd Lt	KIA	O-711502	Navigator	9384	44-10497
700	Henrikson	Henry	J	F/O	KIA	T-124757	Bombardier	9384	44-10497
700	Johnson	Robert	D	T/Sgt	KIA	37472160	Flight Engineer	9384	44-10497
700	O'Keefe	Doyle	L	T/Sgt	POW	36370920	Radio Operator	9384	44-10497

700	Tachovsky	Harry	F	S/Sgt	POW	33830098	Left Waist Gunner	9384	44-10497
700	Loving	John	M	S/Sgt	POW	20820091	Right Waist Gunner	9384	44-10497
700	Galyon	Dwight	F	S/Sgt	POW	38436301	Tail Turret Gunner	9384	44-10497
702	Schaen	James	W	1st Lt	KIA	O-554062	Pilot	9385	44-10511
702	McGough	Bobby	C	2nd Lt	POW	O-1995900	Co-pilot	9385	44-10511
702	Bean	Corman	H	2nd Lt	POW	O-717129	Navigator	9385	44-10511
702	Collar	George	M	2nd Lt	POW	O-703028	Bombardier	9385	44-10511
702	Eppley	George	S	T/Sgt	POW	13091800	Flight Engineer	9385	44-10511
702	Collins	Robert	L	T/Sgt	POW	15130300	Radio Operator	9385	44-10511
702	Parsons	Richard	L	S/Sgt	KIA	32288303	Left Waist Gunner	9385	44-10511
702	Johnson	Edward	J	S/Sgt	KIA	32874288	Right Waist Gunner	9385	44-10511
702	Hurt	Brian	J	S/Sgt	KIA	14052620	Tail Turret Gunner	9385	44-10511

Acknowledgements

The book couldn't have been written without all the help I have received from the following – in no particular order. My apologies if I miss anybody, there have been so many over the years:-

Veterans' verbal accounts:

Reg Miner, Larry Blowers, John Cadden, Ira Weinstein, Art Shay, Eddie Chalfoux, Ed Roloff, Mac MacGregor.

Veterans' written accounts:

Jim Baynham, William Dewey, Leo Pouliot, Frank Bertram, George Collar

William Bruce, Robert Timms, Walter Hassenpflug, Maynard Watson, Eugene George

John French, Doyle O'Keefe, Carroll Snidow.

Veterans video accounts 'Pride of the Nation' courtesy KMHS via Linda Dewey.

Linda Dewey for her father's unpublished manuscript and all the kasselmission.org data

Cathy Barton daughter of 2nd Lieutenant Palmer Bruland

Mona MacGregor English, daughter of 1st Lieutenant Malcolm John MacGregor

Authors Robert Matzen and Scott Culver for their help and advice

Andy Vidion for painstakingly correcting my spelling and grammar

ACKNOWLEDGEMENTS

Librarians at the 2nd Air Division Memorial Library, Norwich

Vivian Rogers Price at the Mighty Eighth Library, Savannah

Mike Simpson at 445bg.org for answering lots of queries

Eberhard Halbig for information on German PoWs, war crimes, crash sites

Erica DeGlopper, Art Shay Archive director for photographs and documents.

Aaron Elson collection of audio cds of veterans' recollections

Norwich Memorial Library's collection of audio recordings

John Davies for his treatise 'Yanks and Little Limeys'

Mike O'Keefe via KMHS.

Kassel Mission Historical Society.

Bibliography

Birsic, Rudolph J., *The history of the 445th Bombardment Group (H) (unofficial)* (1947).

Britain, Tom, *Project Bits and Pieces*

Culver, Scott, *Nine Yanks and a Jerk*, self-published, 2015

Devez, Luc, *Cruel Sky,* self-published, 2015

Elson, Aaron, *King Kong Down,* Chi Chi Press, 2013

Elson, Aaron, *Nine Lives: An oral history*, Chi Chi Press, 1999

Freeman, Roger, *Mighty Eighth War Diary*, Jane's, London. 1984

Harrison, Tom, *Kassel*, Xlibris books, 2013

KMMA, *Kassel Mission reports*, self-published, KMMA inc.

Mastrogiacomo, Sam, *For God and Country*, self-published

Matzen, Robert, *Mission*, Goodnight books, 2016

Robinson, John, *Reason to Live*, Castle books, Memphis, 1988

Terrill, Colonel Robert H., *History of the 445th*

Weinstein, Ira, *The watch that went to War*, Chi Chi Press, 2014

(Courtesy of the Bertram family)

Index

INDEX

177